Family in America

Family in America

Advisory Editors: David J. Rothman
Professor of History,
Columbia University

Sheila M. Rothman

THE

YOUNG WIFE,

OR

DUTIES OF WOMAN IN THE MARRIAGE RELATION

BY WM. A. ALCOTT

*A*RNO *P*RESS & *T*HE *N*EW *Y*ORK *T*IMES
New York 1972

Reprint Edition 1972 by Arno Press Inc.

Reprinted from a copy in
The Wesleyan University Library

LC# 73-169369
ISBN 0-405-03845-3

Family in America
ISBN for complete set: 0-405-03840-2
See last pages of this volume for titles.

Manufactured in the United States of America

THE YOUNG WIFE.

The happiest he! who far from public rage,
                    ... Meek,
Deep in the vale with a choice few retired,
Drinks the pure pleasures of the rural life.
                    THOMSON.

THE
YOUNG WIFE

*by
William A Alcott*

BOSTON:
George W. Light.
1837.

THE YOUNG WIFE,

OR

DUTIES OF WOMAN IN THE MARRIAGE RELATION.

BY WM. A. ALCOTT,

Author of the Young Mother, Young Man's Guide, and House I Live In, and Editor of the Library of Health.

Stereotype Edition.

BOSTON:
GEORGE W. LIGHT, 1 CORNHILL.
1837.

Entered according to Act of Congress, in the year 1837, by WM. A. ALCOTT, in the Clerk's Office of the District Court of Massachusetts.

CONTENTS.

CHAPTER I. GENERAL REMARKS.
Objects of marriage. Duties of a wife. Her importance as an educator. Why . . . . 21—24

CHAPTER II. SUBMISSION.
A common error abroad. Real object of woman. In what respects she is to submit to her husband. Bible doctrine on this subject. Physical inferiority. Concession must be made. Leaving home. Anecdote of a married couple. Caution to the young wife. . 25—32

CHAPTER III. KINDNESS.
Effects of kindness on brute animals—on savages—on children. Case of a father. Effects of kindness on servants and slaves—on a husband. Opinion of Solomon. A new era. Its results to woman. Counsel. Beautiful extracts . . . . 33—40

CHAPTER IV. CHEERFULNESS.
Influence of cheerfulness. Opinion of the Journal of Health. Dr. Salgues' opinion. Interesting anecdote. Evils of a want of cheerfulness. Story of Alexis and Emilia. Reflections . . . . 41—48

CHAPTER V. CONFIDENCE.

Duty of confidence. Married women not always wives. Confiding in gossips. Fault in education. A bad husband not to be given up. Experiment in trusting. We should have but few secrets. . . . . . . 49—52

CHAPTER VI. SYMPATHY.

Scripture doctrine. Miss Edgeworth's opinion—Dr. Rush's. Effects of sympathy. Disposition to vex each other. A caution. Sympathy the first step to improvement. . . . . 53—58

CHAPTER VII. FRIENDSHIP.

Few real friends. Parents not always true friends to children. Anecdote. Stormy period of life. Necessity of a friend. Arrangement of Providence. Woman sent as the friend of man. Wives the truest friends. Four qualifications for this office. Religion considered. Enemies sometimes friends. . . . 59—68

CHAPTER VIII. LOVE.

Is it necessary for love to decline after marriage? Internal love increases. Means of increasing it. Doing good to others makes us love them. Anecdotes; the little girl—the deist. Love, a matter within our own control. General rule. Cautions. . . . . . 69—78

CHAPTER IX. DELICACY AND MODESTY.

Many forms of immodesty. A quotation. Modesty in matrimony. Unchaste language. Example to the husband. Specimens of bad examples. . . . 79—82

CHAPTER X. LOVE OF HOME.

Paul's opinion. Effects of "gadding." Anecdote. Dislike of home. Error in female education. Importance of loving home. A picture drawn by Solomon. Two pictures by Abbott. Effects of loving home on the family. Hints to the reader. The Family Monitor. 83—96

CHAPTER XI. SELF-RESPECT.

A principle. Self-respect should be early cultivated. An anecdote. . . . . 97—100

CHAPTER XII. PURITY OF CHARACTER.

Explanation of the term. Impurity of character very common. Case of Lucius and Emilia. Seduction. The consequences. Several hints. . . . . 101—107

CHAPTER XIII. SIMPLICITY.

Simplicity a virtue. Very rare. Simplicity of language. Story of Mrs. L. Simplicity of conduct. . . 108—112

CHAPTER XIV. NEATNESS.

Great importance of neatness. Want of it. Effects on the husband. Neatness in small matters. Structure of the skin. Necessity of bathing. Effect of neatness on morals. Effect of example. Difficulties considered. How to train a husband to slovenliness. Want of neatness in little things. . . . . 113—121

CHAPTER XV. ORDER AND METHOD.

Order, heaven's first law. Importance to the housekeeper. Book-learning. Prejudices against it. Story of Fidelia. Consequences of disorder. . . . 122—125

CHAPTER XVI PUNCTUALITY.

Punctuality lengthens life—is indispensable. Its influence on others. Various forms of punctuality. Anecdote. Reflections. Case of the farmer. The wife's excuses. Real state of the case. Appeal to those whom it concerns. . . . . 126—134

CHAPTER XVII. EARLY RISING.

The young wife should rise early. Means of forming the habit. Retire early—with a quiet stomach—a quiet mind. Resolve strongly. Early training. Mr. and Mrs. Clifford. Samuel Sidney. Reflections. 135—146

CHAPTER XVIII. INDUSTRY.

An anecdote. Motives to industry. Bible examples of this virtue. . . . . 147—151

CHAPTER XIX. DOMESTIC ECONOMY.

Economy a word of broad meaning. Much of this chapter anticipated. Servants—their general employment to be regretted. Spirit of the times—illustrated by an anecdote. American nobles. Servants cannot always be dispensed with. Seven reasons for avoiding them, if possible. 1. They are unnecessary. 2. Costly. 3. Break in upon the order of families. 4. Create distinctions in society. 5. Are bad teachers. 6. Practice anti-republican. 7. It is unchristian. Waste of time in cookery. What useful cookery is. Other wasteful practices. Morning calls. General remarks. An, anecdote. . . . . 152—177

CHAPTER XX. DOMESTIC REFORM.

Present state of things. Females ignorant of domestic concerns. A great mistake in education. Nature

CONTENTS. 9

of the mistake. Cause of the pecuniary distress of our country. Example of ministers. Change or reform necessary. How it is to be effected. By whom begun. The young wife to begin it. She should begin immediately. One serious difficulty. How to overcome it. Gradual reformation. Rapid progress, ultimately. Book learning. How far books are useful. " The Frugal Housewife." " Bread and Bread-making." 178—191

CHAPTER XXI. SOBRIETY.

Definition of the term. Something more than temperance. Tea drinking. Effects of tea and coffee. Physiology of their effects. Nervous excitement—compared with intoxication. Proofs of the author's views. Sobriety at feasts. Sobriety in company. Other forms of sobriety. . . . . 192—199

CHAPTER XXII. DISCRETION.

Paul's estimate of the importance of discretion. Opinions of Gisborne. Various forms of indiscretion. Danger of extremes. What true purity is. A word of caution to the indiscreet. . . . . 200—204

CHAPTER XXIII. SCOLDING.

Many kinds of scolds. Internal scolding. Intermittent scolds. Periodical scolding. Other forms of scolding. Hints over the husband's shoulder. 205—207

CHAPTER XXIV. FORBEARANCE.

Perfection not to be expected. Maxim of a philosopher. Spirit of forbearance a pearl of great price. Cases where forbearance is required. Triumphing, " I told you so." Comparisons. Joking. Saying of Salzman. . . . . 208—212

CHAPTER XXV. CONTENTMENT.

Value of contentment. Why it is especially valuable to the young wife. Duty to her own family and others. Duty to God. . . . . 213—217

CHAPTER XXVI. HABITS AND MANNERS.

Little things. Setting out in life. Important to set out right. Difficulty with some husbands. How to manage. Eugene and Juliet. General principles. 218—221

CHAPTER XXVII. DRESS.

Opinion of Paul. Real objects of dress. Modesty. Dress should regulate our temperature. Frequent change—why useful. General rule. A painful sight. Nature of profuse perspiration, or sweating. Material of dress. Objections to cotton. Fashion of dress. Compression of the lungs—its evils. Sympathies. Moderate indulgence. Hiding defects by dress. Dress of the husband. . . . . 222—244

CHAPTER XXVIII. HEALTH.

Purity of the air in our apartments. Purity of clothing—furniture—cellars—drains—wells, &c. Personal cleanliness. Its expense not to be considered. Various modes of exercise. Household labor. Exercise in the open air. Walking. Riding. Health, in our own keeping. The husband's health. General remarks. 245—256

CHAPTER XXIX. ATTENDING THE SICK.

Attending the sick should be a part of female education. Objections to this view considered. Reasons why females should be thus trained. Their native qualifications for this office. Their labor cheaper. They have stronger sympathies. Application of the principle to the case of the young wife. . . . . 257—264

CHAPTER XXX. LOVE OF INFANCY AND CHILDHOOD.

What the love of childhood is. Frequent want of it. Dr. Gregory's opinion—Mr. Addison's. Great gulf fixed between children and adults. Love of childhood favorable to mental improvement—to the happiness of the wife—to the happiness of her husband—to religious improvement. Example of the Saviour. How to elicit this love, when it is wanting. Remarks on faith. What faith can enable us to accomplish. 265—273

CHAPTER XXXI. GIVING ADVICE.

Advice of females in regard to business. Why it is often undervalued. Objections answered. How far advice is applicable. Advice in manners and morals. Advice in religion. . . . . 274—283

CHAPTER XXXII. SELF-GOVERNMENT.

Difficulties of self-government. Meaning of the term. Error in education. What is to be done? Motive to be presented. Directions how to proceed. Co-operation of the husband. The results happy. 284—291

CHAPTER XXXIII. INTELLECTUAL IMPROVEMENT.

Anecdote of Mrs. H. Course of study after marriage. Much of it excellent. Cooperation of the husband and wife. Nature of education. Difficulties of studying in married life. They may be overcome. Importance of system. Evils of a want of it. Anecdote. Chemistry. Its importance illustrated. Terrible consequences of ignorance in housewifery. Much poisoning in the community. Study of other sciences. Anatomy and physiology. A few books recommended. Collateral topics of study. Knowledge necessary to benevolent effort. Study of the subject of education. Errors. Theory and experience. . . . . . 292—326

CHAPTER XXXIV. SOCIAL IMPROVEMENT.

Anecdote of Alcibiades. Intention of the Creator. Marriage of course a social state. Morning calls. Evening visits. Excitements. Balls and theatres. Visiting in the afternoon. Social advantages of large families. Visiting by large companies. Topics of conversation. Scandal. Opposition of human nature to the gospel. Reading at social meetings. An important caution. . . . . 327—338

CHAPTER XXXV. MORAL AND RELIGIOUS IMPROVEMENT.

Doing good. Many forms of doing good. Philosophy of doing good. Associated effort. How to select societies. Individual charitable effort. The poor. The ignorant. The vicious. The sick. Caution in regard to visiting the sick. Prayer as a means of improvement. Self-examination. Reading. The Bible. Other useful books. . . . . 339—350

CHAPTER XXXVI. MORAL INFLUENCE ON THE HUSBAND.

Mode of female influence on the husband. Mr. Flint's encomium. Examples of female influence. Wife of

Jonathan Edwards—of Sir James Mackintosh. True position of woman in society. Serious error of some modern writers. A caution. Making haste to be rich. A species of mania. Its extent and evils. How the young wife is concerned with it. What she can do to remove it. Agur's prayer—seldom used in modern times. Particular modes of female influence. Office seeking. How to dissuade from it. Exposures to intemperance. Female consistency. Female piety. Its effects on the husband—compared with amiableness and beauty. Apparent objection to the writer's views. Woman's prerogative. . . . . . 351—376

PREFACE.

Conversing, one day, with the author of a popular series of books, I told him I objected to his last work because it was incomplete. I acknowledge the fault you mention, he replied, but what would you have had me do? I said all I knew on the subject. Would you have an author, for the sake of rendering his book complete, tell what he does not know?

This reply afforded me a valuable hint, and I resolved to profit from it. If all which authors *do not know* were erased from their books, how many ponderous volumes would sink at once to the size of pamphlets, and how greatly would the bulk of nearly all be diminished?

It is not the object of the following work to give a complete view of the duties of a young wife. My purpose has been simply to present my own views on a few points—such as have been the subjects of much observation and reflection—and to dwell at considerable length on them, leaving the rest to other writers. There is no want of the latter; we have more than one " Young Wife's Book " already extant; and along with some defects, each of them doubtless has its excellencies. It is probably a transcript of the author's mind on this great and important subject; and is hence more or less perfect according to the extent of his observation, and his knowledge of the nature of those whom he has observed. I have never read but one of them, however, and that only partly through. Whatever may be the merits or demerits of the following volume, it is principally original. For the few extracts I have made, I have given, in every instance, so far as I know, sufficient credit.

It may also be proper to observe, in regard to some of the views which I have ventured to present in reference to the appropriate sphere and duties of woman in matrimonial life, that every chapter of this work was written many months before the appearance of certain recent publications involving, in some respects, similar sentiments This statement may, it is confessed, be deemed unnecessary. It is soon enough, it may be thought, to repel the charge of plagiarism, when it has actually been made. And whatever may have been the excellencies or defects of any former volumes, prepared by the author, he has not as yet incurred the charge of following too closely in the track of others.

In pursuing my subject, however, I have not always confined myself to the more obvious and generally admitted qualifications and duties which a new and interesting and important relation imposes upon the young wife, but have sometimes treated at large on several topics which are not only of great importance to her as a member of the human family, but whose importance, trained as she usually is, in comparative ignorance, is greatly enhanced by the position she sustains to her husband and her other friends. In a word, I have endeavored to take her to be precisely what in the present state of things a wife is, and to give such advice and instruction as, in my own view, she needs for the better discharge of her varied duties to herself, her husband and others.

Let me caution the reader against one mistake into which she may be liable to fall. In dwelling at length, as I sometimes do, on the duties of a wife, it may be thought that I impose too heavy a burden on her, and too little on the husband. For example, in speaking of the duty of submission, it may be supposed by some, at first view, that I would render man a sort of petty tyrant. But let it be remembered that I am not writing, in this volume, for the husband directly, but for the wife ; and that however weighty, or important, or responsible the duties of the former may be, those of the latter are by no means the less so on account of my silence respecting the husband. Even in regard to concession and submission, the fact that these duties, especially the former, often devolve on the husband as well as the wife, does not at all lessen the obligations of the latter. The liability of being misunderstood, to which I refer, is inseparable, perhaps, from the practice of writing for particular classes of society ; and if so, every author must be prepared to meet it.

I have one more caution. If the same idea or truth should sometimes appear more than once, in the following pages, let it not be regarded as mere repetition, but rather as presented in a new light to show its aspect, bearings, or relations, as viewed from some other point, or considered in some other connection. There are no repetitions but what are intended, either to reiterate or illustrate what are deemed important sentiments.

Boston, October, 1837.

THE YOUNG WIFE.

CHAPTER I.

GENERAL REMARKS.

Objects of marriage. Duties of a wife. Her importance as an educator. Why.

THE objects of the marriage institution may all be comprised under two general heads. First, the education of the parties concerned; second, the education of those committed to their care. It will be obvious, however, that the word education, thus used, includes much more than mere instruction in knowledge. The term is used in its largest sense, as implying and including everything which forms character for this world or the world to come.

If the view I have here taken of the intention of marriage be correct—and I think it will be found to accord both with reason and revelation—then we see, at once, what is the leading duty of the young wife, considered merely as such, and what are the ends which she should propose. She is to be, in one word, "a help-meet" to her husband. She is to assist him—cooperate with him—in the work of self-education. The education of others, however important a duty of the married life it may ultimately become, belongs to the Young Mother rather than to the Young Wife, and will therefore only be made an incidental or occasional subject of discussion in the present volume.

Every day educates us for every day which follows it, and indeed for every subsequent period of our existence, because all the various events, and circumstances, and employments of each day contribute to form the future character. Just in proportion, then, as the wife can modify or control these circumstances, events and employments in her family, just in the same proportion is she an educator of her husband. This education may, indeed, be either good or bad, according to the spirit and manner in which it is conducted; but educate at some rate or other, the wife always must, in all she says or does in the presence of others—I had almost said, in all she thinks and feels. She is moreover the most efficient of all the educators of her husband, because her influence is so constant. It also happens that in no way can she so rapidly promote her own improvement, as in promoting that of her husband; since the light and influence which she sheds on him is necessarily reflected upon herself.

These remarks apply with most force, it is true, to the *young* wife, as my title would indicate. But they are also applicable, in no small degree, to those who are more advanced in years. The power of persons, places, events and circumstances, to form or reform human character, is in exactly an inverse proportion, other things being equal, to our age. The younger the parties are, when they enter into wedlock, the more they can do, mutually, in the great work of self-improvement. But something can be done, as long as life lasts. There is no age at which the work of human education ceases. Character is forming for the great future, till we pass the bounds of time and space, and enter a world where retribution predominates rather than trial—a world where character remains fixed—a world of universal and never ending manhood.

Let it not be hastily supposed that I expect the wife to do much by means of set lessons, or in any of the more direct forms of what is commonly called education; though she is not to remain wholly inefficient, even in this respect, as will be seen in another place. But it is by conduct and example that she is to effect most, in the education of her husband. It is by indirect means—silent, gentle, and often unperceived, but always operative. The growth of the vegetable world is not so much effected by the bright meridian glare of heaven's resplendent luminary, and by the violent rain and the tempest, as by the milder light of morning and evening, the gentler breezes, the soft descending showers, and the still more softly distilling dew. In like manner is it the province of woman to accomplish most for human advancement, and above all in her own family, by indirect if not by silent efforts. She is to teach, at least in no small degree, as though she taught not. She is to perform the duties of her office, not like the king of day, but rather like the paler empress of night, in so unperceived a manner as to leave it doubtful whether she has any influence or not, except by the general law of attraction.

Having thus stated, as briefly as possible, some of the principles which form the basis of this work, I proceed to consider, in a series of chapters, the various means by which the young wife is to accomplish most successfully the purpose of her mission.

CHAPTER II.

SUBMISSION.

A common error abroad. Real object of woman. In what respects she is to submit to her husband. Bible doctrine on this subject. Physical inferiority. Concession must be made. Leaving home. Anecdote of a married couple. Caution to the young wife.

An opinion still prevails, even in civilized countries, that woman should be little more than the mere instrument of her husband; that on many points she is not expected to have a voice; that she should have even no opinion; and that her duty consists in submitting, without a question, to the dictates of her "lord."

Now I am of opinion that woman is made to supply, in some measure, the defects in her husband's character—thus making him a more perfect man than otherwise he would be. But I hold, also, that the same duty is required of the husband toward the wife, and with the same view and end; and that in this respect, the husband has little, if indeed any superiority. I hold, moreover, that God has required of each party, in the married state, though the union be ever so close or so perfect, to preserve the individual character of each. No female has a right, were she disposed to do it, so to merge her own character in that of her husband, as to lose her own individuality.

Still I cannot help thinking that there is a species of submission to the husband sometimes required of the wife. Not that I would ever claim it myself, or recommend to any one else to make the claim. If a wife has not good sense enough to yield, voluntarily, what I suppose ought to be yielded, it is probably of little importance for the husband to claim anything. Perhaps I would say, "That is my opinion; you will, of course, do or act as you please."

And yet something of submission is certainly due. There was a time, in the history of our world, when woman did not exist. Man was not only alone—without a companion—but destitute of a "help-meet"—an assistant. In these circumstances, almighty Power called forth, and, as it would seem, for this very purpose, that modified, and in some respects improved form of humanity, to which was afterwards given the name of woman, and *presented her to man.* She was to be man's assistant.

This distinction is recognized throughout the Bible. Man is always considered as the head of the family, and woman as the helper. The man is not created for the woman—so the matter is represented—but the woman for the man.

It is true that this does not, of necessity, imply an intellectual and moral inferiority on the part of woman. It does not preclude the idea that in morals she may even be the superior. The concession is that of physical prowess, rather than of moral influence.

It is a concession, however, whose necessity stands as prominent in the pages of the great book of nature as in those of revelation. The exercise of that physical force which seems necessary in many of the arts and employments of life, is scarcely compatible with woman's distinguishing characteristics and her peculiar prerogative, had it been assigned her.

Heaven has accordingly withheld it. No form of education will give to woman a masculine development. No circumstances will impart to her muscular system, as a whole, that power which is so constantly developed in the other sex. Even in those countries, and among those tribes, where the ruder and coarser employments have been partially or wholly allotted her, she still retains the more striking physical traits of character which God in nature has assigned. They may indeed be modified, slightly, but never wholly overcome.

A skilful anatomist could still distinguish the sexes, at any age, by a mere hasty inspection of an arm or a face, after the lapse of a thousand successive generations.

Let me not hence be set down as an enemy to female athletic exercises. What muscular exercise, in degree, woman does demand, is demanded still more imperiously than in man. She needs muscular exercise during her growth and after maturity, both to develope her form, internal and external, and to maintain her health. But no muscular exercise whatever—and this is the burden of my present argument—will essentially and permanently alter her structure, to render it more masculine in future generations. Say what we will, therefore, God in nature must have imposed on her a physical inferiority. She is thus obviously fitted to be an assistant to her husband in the work of self-improvement, and the improvement of others.

Perhaps all this inquiry is utterly needless. Perhaps very few readers entertain a single doubt on any one of these points. But it was necessary to make the statement, preliminary to what follows in other chapters.

Indeed, in one point, the agitation of this question would certainly seem needless. Matrimony cannot exist, without concession on both sides. Each party gives up certain natural rights, for the sake of certain privileges to be acquired. On which side lies the balance of concession, we need not inquire; it is sufficient if it is shown that it must be made, and that matrimony cannot exist without it.

I say, then, that the very act of entering into the married state is, on the part of the woman, a concession. It matters little whether this fact is recognized in the external forms of celebrating this rite or not; it is essential to, and inherent in its nature.

Leaving home, as a general rule, involves concession and submission. What female ever quits the circle in which she is brought up, in the expectation of retaining every privilege and every right to which she has been accustomed? Does she not, on the contrary, even diminish her own personal enjoyment?

In addition to the physical comforts of which she voluntarily deprives herself, does she not subject herself to numerous cares, and responsibilities, and trials? Does she not submit, at least prospectively, to a long train of circumstances and consequences which, in her father's house, she would be able to escape? Does she not even merge her own name in that of her husband? And is there no concession in all this? Is there no submission?

How much soever of his own natural rights the husband is required to yield, the concessions of the wife are still more numerous, and justify the inevitable conclusion that matrimony involves, as a matter of the plainest necessity, not only a greater degree of dependence on her part, but also a species of inferiority.

Let me here say again, that I would be the last person in the world to justify a tyrannical assumption of superiority on the part of our own sex. Let nothing be claimed by man, except what the necessity of the circumstances requires; and let even this be done in the most gentle manner. But if reason, nature and revelation unite in affirming that the balance of concession does actually devolve on woman, it is proper to say so. I may also add, that the more cheerful and voluntary the submission, the happier the results.

This was the conclusion of a newly married couple, among my own acquaintance. Each respected the rights of the other, but both saw how much more numerous the points were in which woman was required to yield; and both saw, too, the necessity of an umpire, in certain cases. It was therefore mutually agreed that it belonged to the husband to decide, in all matters of dispute. This point, once settled, has never, thus far, been questioned by either party.

SUBMISSION.

But besides the numerous general concessions which a well regulated matrimonial state requires of the wife, and which, from its very nature, it involves, she is called to a series of smaller concessions, on which depend, much more than on all else, her comfort and happiness.

No woman can suppose herself perfect in opinions, habits or manners. But whether hers are right or wrong, she finds them daily, and perhaps hourly conflicting with those of her husband. He has been trained differently from herself. He has been accustomed to view things through a medium somewhat different. He is more ignorant on many points than she; and it unfortunately happens that when a difference of opinion arises among mankind—and between husband and wife, no less than elsewhere—those who are most ignorant will usually be most positive, and most tenacious of their sentiments.

He is often more tenacious of habits and manners than of opinions; and especially of small habits. But what shall be done? Shall she set herself firmly against every habit which she has reason to believe is not the very best? Shall she not rather, for the sake of peace, often concede or yield a point, at least for the time?

Perhaps there is no one thing on which domestic happiness so much depends as this; here, too, as in the matters already mentioned, the balance of concession devolves on the wife. Whether the husband concede or not, she must. If she insists too long or too strenuously for what she deems to be truth or right in small matters, she does it at the expense of her own comfort and peace. I do not say that she must express her assent to what she does not believe; but I do say that she must not dispute too long about it. She must endeavor to waive the whole subject. By contending, she will probably gain nothing, but only confirm him in his habits or opinions. By a temporary concession, that is, by suspending the question, she may possibly lead him to reflect farther, and to change his views or conduct.

So valuable is the disposition to make temporary concessions in matters of opinion or habit, that an aged friend of mine, in giving directions in reference to matrimony prior to marriage, represented the whole question of domestic happiness or misery as turning upon this single point. After giving the reasons for her opinions, she concluded by observing—" If you are both wise in this respect, you cannot but be prosperous and happy."

CHAPTER III.

KINDNESS.

Effects of kindness on brute animals—on savages—on children. Case of a father. Effects of kindness on servants and slaves—on a husband. Opinion of Solomon. A new era. Its results to woman. Counsel. Beautiful extracts.

CONSTANT and unremitted kindness is irresistible. I say this with the more confidence, from the effect which experience has shown that it has on the insane and the idiotic, and even on beasts. I do not believe there is an animal on earth that can wholly resist its influence.

I have watched the effects of kindness on the noble horse, the patient ox, the domestic cat and dog, and even the grovelling pig. I have read of its effects on the elephant, the camel, the lama, and indeed on almost every known animal—even the fierce lion, and the savage hyena; and I have usually found those effects obvious. The best domestic animals I have ever seen were reared by kind and merciful masters; the worst by those of a contrary disposition.

Kindness to an animal, and even to men, may not, it is true, always change, at once, habits or character. Our kindness to a savage will not, of necessity, render him civilized;—it may, indeed, leave him as much of a savage as he was before. But it will, at the least, increase his love for us, and his confidence in us, so that the more appropriate or more efficient means of changing or meliorating his condition can be successfully applied. Kindness, though it should overcome the criminal, may not reform him; but it will almost inevitably place him in a condition in which other means for his reformation can be applied.

Nothing secures the love and confidence of children like unremitted kindness. Do what else you will to them, if the general tenor of your life indicate a kind heart and kind feelings towards them, you are sure of their affection, and may lead them almost whithersoever you will.

I know a father who is sometimes fretful and peevish; and I have occasionally seen him in a rage. When he is so, his whole family feel the effects of it; sometimes—all but the wife—in blows. Yet this is not the general tenor of his life. He is, for the most part, the kind husband, and the tender and affectionate father. His periods of fretfulness or rage are but as the occasional storm in a land of serenity and sunshine; and are regarded as such by the family. They dread them, indeed, and sometimes endeavor to shelter themselves from their effects; but they know the storm will soon be over.

Now these moral storms are far from being as salutary as the physical storm;—nay, they are in themselves a most serious evil. But they are far from being the worst evil that could befall a family. I honestly believe that an occasional fit of rage does less mischief than a settled gloom; just as an occasional storm injures vegetation less than to have the sun constantly obscured. In the case I have just mentioned, the wife is on the whole happy, and the children very affectionate and tolerably well educated, notwithstanding the father's occasional sallies.

The master, too, seldom fails to discover the effect of kindness on his servant or slave, and to govern himself accordingly. I have known an instance of such severity in a slaveholder towards favorite slaves, as I thought at the time could not fail wholly to estrange their hearts from him. And yet they loved him scarcely the less for it, because it was rather an occasional thing, and not in keeping with the general tenor of his conduct.

But if these are the effects of remitted kindness—if not only savage men but fierce animals are susceptible of its influence—if, in one word, its influence is irresistible—then how important it is that it should be constantly brought to bear, in a relation of all others the nearest and most tender! If the occasional violence of man does not wholly destroy its legitimate tendency, what happy results would not follow its uninterrupted influence on the part of woman, in married life!

There can be no room for doubt on this subject. There is reason to believe that the simple exercise of kindness, in the most intimate and unremitted relations of matrimonial life, would do more to promote domestic bliss than the wisest have ever yet supposed. The husband can, in this respect, do much; but the wife can do more—much more. Can there be a doubt that what is so important to domestic happiness, and through that, so promotive of the general good, is demanded? May it not be here assumed that kindness, next to concession, is the first and most imperative of the young wife's duties?

Solomon, in his description of a virtuous wife, couples kindness with wisdom, and considers his picture incomplete without it. "She openeth her mouth with wisdom," says he; but as if this were not enough, he immediately adds, "and in her tongue is the law of kindness."

The time has been, in the history of our world, when it was governed chiefly by physical force.

But a new order of things is coming about, and men are beginning to be controlled by a moral influence. It is scarcely necessary to say that whatever may have been or may continue to be hereafter the sub-agents in effecting this great revolution, the great and principal agent is christianity.

While the world was ruled by physical force, and woman—and even the wife—was regarded as only a better sort of menial, human improvement was slow. It was so, especially, because so little was done in the family—the great cradle of character. Yet there was something done, even here; and whatever was achieved of human melioration seemed to be the effect of maternal love.

It was reserved, however, for a new era—one upon which we are now entering—to show the silent power which woman has in governing the world. Her influence is just now beginning to be felt. The nations, instead of being controlled by fear, are ere long to be controlled by the law of love and kindness. In this change—revolution I have called it—woman is to perform a most important, if not the principal part. She is to wield the sceptre, first over her husband, and next over the children whom God may give her.

Let her understand, then, fully, the efficacy of kindness, in enabling her to fulfil her duty and destiny. Let her be particularly careful to be kind in the smaller matters. It is no hard task to maintain kind feelings amid the great concerns of life, and while we are nerved and braced for the work. It is no difficult task to preserve the occasional look and tone and word and action of kindness and love; but to preserve our souls, as we ought, when entirely off our guard, at home, in the domestic circle, and to do this always, is not so easy a matter. And yet this is precisely what is most necessary to be done. It is in vain, or almost in vain, to hope for any signal amelioration of our race, through family influence, till this point is secured—till woman's life, amid her household, is one uninterrupted series of kind actions, words, tones and gestures, and till she has overcome and transformed her husband. This is one peculiar and pressing duty of the young wife; and it is a duty which ought in no circumstances to be overlooked or disregarded.

This kindness must extend even to what are called little things. Mrs. Sprout, in her "Family Lectures," has the following highly interesting remarks on this subject:

"A great portion of the misery which has so often embittered married life, I am persuaded has originated in the neglect of trifles. Connubial happiness is a thing of too fine a texture to be handled roughly. It is a plant which will not even bear the touch of unkindness—a delicate flower, which indifference will chill, and suspicion blast. It must be watered with the showers of attention, and guarded with the impregnable barrier of unshaken confidence. In this way, it will bloom with fragrance in every season of life, and sweeten even the loneliness of declining years."

I am not over-fond of quotations, however apropos; but since I have begun to quote, allow me to finish this chapter with a few excellent things which I have found in the course of my reading on this subject.

In the "Whisper to a Newly Married Pair," I find the following paragraph. It is, to say the least, worth reading once :

"I repeat, it is amazing how trifles—the most insignificant trifles—even a word, even a look—yes, truly, a look, a glance—completely possess the power, at times, of either pleasing or displeasing. Let this sink deep into your mind ; remember that to endeavor to keep a husband in constant good humor is one of the first duties of a wife."

"Our lives," says an intelligent writer, "are made up of little things. If the neglect of little duties is a source of unhappiness, they at once lose their insignificancy. If little peculiarities of manner, of expression or habit, are annoying, they are of sufficient importance to claim the attention, and demand the amendment of every well-inclined individual.

"Many a well-meaning wife may trace the coldness and estrangement of her husband to some trifling cause. If a husband, for example, says, 'Do n't put your feet upon the grate,' the subject is of sufficient importance to induce you to guard against a repetition. His taste is annoyed by the least inelegance of attitude.

"But it is not errors like these—errors observed, perhaps, only by the extremely refined—to which I would particularly advert; it is the disregard of that inestimable rule—'Do as you wish to be done by'—a rule applicable to every situation of every individual, capable of being applied to the greatest and most momentous subjects, as well as to the most simple affairs of household propriety—a rule comprising within itself a motive for action, which, if it were universally observed, would supersede the necessity of legislation, and banish unhappiness from the world. This simple yet important rule is of itself sufficient to establish the divine character of him who uttered it. He or she who wantonly disregards this divine rule, even in little things, is sapping the very foundation of domestic happiness."

CHAPTER IV.

CHEERFULNESS.

Influence of cheerfulness. Opinion of the Journal of Health. Dr. Salgues' opinion. Interesting anecdote. Evils of a want of cheerfulness. Story of Alexis and Emilia. Reflections.

THE young wife also owes it to her husband and to the world, to be cheerful. She is seldom aware of the amazing importance of this quality to her own happiness, as well as to that of others.

In the second volume of the Journal of Health, there is an extended essay on the importance of cheerfulness to health and longevity. Nor is it a solitary instance. Many writers, both in morals and medicine, have dwelt, at considerable length, on its favorable tendency on our every-day happiness.

Dr. Salgues, professor to the Institute of France, has the following excellent remarks on the importance of what he calls gaiety, but which answers exactly to what we call cheerfulness:—" It is," says he, " the best preservative against anxiety and grief; it is the golden panacea, the secret of longevity, the elixir of life." And in another place, he adds, "Joy and gaiety give activity to transpiration, render digestion easier and better, sleep more regular and refreshing, the cure of sickness easier, the period of convalescence shorter, and life itself longer."

This is the importance of cheerfulness in general. But its peculiar importance to the wife can best be seen by observing those families where it is wanting. Unhappily, they are so numerous that we need not go very far for the purpose.

I recollect most distinctly a family of this painful description, not a hundred miles from the place of my nativity.

It was a small family, in moderate, though not affluent circumstances, and surrounded by most of those externals which are calculated to make life delightful. Yet cheerfulness was only an occasional visitor there—seldom or never an inmate.

The father labored like a galley slave, to amass property, and almost always came home from his labor fatigued and dejected; never smiling or happy. The mother, born, as it seemed, to perpetual sullenness and gloom, did nothing, of course, to cheer his spirits. Not a sprightly word or cheering look was ever transmitted from the one to the other, except on extraordinary occasions, as on the arrival of some friendly visitor. More than this, the countenance of the mother usually wore a frown, even in her happiest moments.

In this sad condition things went on for many years. A family of three children were in the mean time rising to maturity, and their character, for time and for eternity, forming under such woful influences. They were at length fairly on the stage of life, and actors in life's busy scenes. And what were their tempers and dispositions? Two of them are far from being cheerful or happy. Nor were they happy in their youth; for they were often melancholic in the midst of the gayest companions. Some of them already have rising families of their own, among whom they are spreading, by gloomy countenances, the same unhappy influences to which themselves, in early life, had been subjected.

In my youth I had occasion to spend a few days in the cheerless family of which I have been speaking. As I was a mere boy, there was probably no effort to appear differently from what was usual in the family; and therefore I had a fine opportunity to see things as they were.

I believe I was in the family four days. Yet during this whole time, I never heard a pleasant voice, or saw a kind countenance or a friendly smile, except in a single instance. The father was dejected; the mother was irritable; the daughters were peevish and gloomy; the son was discontented and unhappy.

There were no cords of love and union there. The father never sat down, in the midst of a happy family, nor formed the hero of a circle around the fireside. If he had a moment's leisure, he was at the "store," or the "corner," in the midst of other and sometimes more unfavorable influences.

Now when I reflect upon the circumstances of this group of relatives—for I will not call it a family—I feel a good degree of confidence that maternal kindness would have prevented all this. Not through the medium of occasional smiles or acts of kindness, but by an uninterrupted series of those looks and acts that make their impression on the heart, and imperceptibly, though effectually, win it.

Abbott, in his "Path of Peace," describes this state of things as if he too, like myself, had been an eye witness to it. Speaking of the want of cheerfulness, and its sad effects on the husband, he thus observes:

"When, wearied and excited by the harassments of the day, your husband has returned to his home, he has not been met with a smile of welcome, and a placid heart. The parlor is in a clutter, the children are neglected, his wife is fretful. Love, even the most pure and the most fervent, cannot long survive such encounters. The tavern-keeper will bid him welcome. He will have the little snug parlor, for the whist party, neat and in order, and his associates will be careful to avoid offence. They will greet him with the open hand and the smiling brow. Is it strange, that a man who is not governed by christian principle, should, under such circumstances, forget his wife and forsake his home? Is it strange, that he should live with those who are careful to minister to his pleasures?"

He also gives the following excellent advice:

"Cultivate a cheerful spirit. Cheerfulness is the twin sister of gratitude. They are born together. They walk hand in hand through life, and the death of the one breaks the heart of the other. Gratitude is the homage which the heart gives to God for his goodness. Cheerfulness is the external manifestation of this praise."

I have said that the importance of cheerfulness in a wife could best be shown, by exhibiting the evils which flow from a want of it. But it may also be shown by examples of the contrary description. I will present one.

Alexis is a day laborer. He was originally indolent; but the wants of a family, beginning to be felt, have aroused him. He now labors incessantly, and labors hard.

In all his efforts, he is seconded and sustained by his wife. It is true she was a little disappointed in her expectations in regard to his circumstances. As he was the son of a wealthy farmer, she thought he would receive that aid from his father which would at least render their circumstances comfortable. But no: the old gripus withholds his aid, to a dollar. He will not lift a finger to encourage. "Let him put his own shoulder to the wheel, and then call for Hercules."—I like the principle very well, but I should like it also if the old man was sincere in his application of it—if it were not a mere excuse for retaining, at its full size, his own heap.

But as I have already intimated, Emilia, though a little disappointed, is not discouraged. She makes the best of things as they are. She is doing her utmost. And she is doing very much. She has indeed already done much. She has led Alexis into habits of industry, already; she is now leading him to other virtues, and to happiness.

And how is she doing it? Not by wise words, in the form of direct instruction;—not by her sage counsels;—not even by her example, alone. What then? It is by her never-tiring cheerfulness; or at least chiefly so.

How is this cheerfulness shown or manifested? To answer this question fully would be to give the whole history of a day. I need only say that her countenance always wears a smile, an unaffected one, too, when she meets him ; and that her every word or action corresponds to the feelings indicated by her countenance. Everything she says or does in his presence warms his heart, and inspires hope. And to inspire hope is to reform and to make happy.

Above all, does she perform her angelic task by the reception she gives him at evening. When he comes home, as often happens, after dark, he finds not only the lighted window and the blazing hearth, but the still more cheering light of his wife's countenance, to welcome him.

He can scarcely feel a want of food, drink or repose, which is not fully anticipated, and for which provision is not made in the most happy manner. Who that is perpetually cheered by those whom he tenderly loves, can help being cheerful? Who can help smiling, that is constantly smiled upon? Who can avoid being happy, where nought exists but happiness?

Had Alexis married any other than Emilia, or a person who, like her, sympathized deeply with him, and had she proved a very angel to him in every other respect, it is doubtful whether he would ever have made the industrious man he now is. Nay, more ; there is every reason to believe he would have gone "down hill" with a velocity far greater than that with which he is now moving upwards.

Emilia has saved him. She has led him, through a kind and merciful providence, into the right way. His path, if it be not that of the just, in the scripture sense of the phrase, is at least like it; and is probably destined, like it, to shine brighter and brighter unto the perfect day.

CHAPTER V.

CONFIDENCE.

Duty of confidence. Married women not always wives. Confiding in gossips. Fault in education. A bad husband not to be given up. Experiment in trusting. We should have but few secrets.

It may seem idle to suggest to a wife the duty of confiding in her husband. She has evinced her confidence in him, it will be said, by marrying him. Has she not entrusted him with everything dear to her this side of the grave, excepting perhaps the destiny of her immortal spirit? And shall she now be advised to put confidence in him?

But as there are those who bear the name, who are not husbands, so there are to be found married women who are not wives. They have not entire confidence in their husbands, after all. They only confide in them in part. They trust them to a certain extent. Still there is a string of secrets behind, which they dare not communicate, even to them.

I will not say that a wife should bury nothing in her own breast. I will not say that things may not transpire, both before and after marriage, which it were better to lock up in one's own bosom forever. It may be even so. It probably is so. But I do say that if a married lady has a bosom friend at all—if she confides her inmost secrets to any one—it should be to her husband. She has no right to trust some secret-loving gossip with that which she dares not, for her very life, confide to her husband.

Do you say that some husbands are not worthy of being confided in, or trusted? I know they are not, and it is a most unhappy circumstance; and if your husband is of this description, I pity you. But what is to be done? You have married him, and you cannot go back. You have made him your husband; ought you not now to treat him as such?

Let me observe that there is a fault here, in our system of early education. Children are not taught to be trusted. There is no way of rendering people worthy of being confided in, or trusted, but by reposing confidence in them. The work should be commenced early. Let a child be early taught to keep a secret. Repose confidence in him, again and again, till you make him worthy of your confidence.

Were this advice followed, we should not find so many persons laying claim to the sacred names of husband and wife, who are yet unwilling to keep a secret, and unworthy of confidence. We should not find the wife so often telling Mrs. A. B. something which she would not, for the world, tell her own husband.

But taking a husband, too, of the worst stamp, in this respect, I do think he ought not to be deemed irreclaimable. I shall hereafter insist on it, as a sacred and important duty of the wife, to improve his character physically, intellectually, socially, morally and religiously. All I have to say on this point here is, that it will be one important item in this great work, to teach him to be worthy of her confidence.

There is a tendency in our natures to become what we are taken to be. Take your husband to be worthy of being trusted, and commit a secret or something else to his keeping. Let it be, if possible, of such a character or nature that it will be for his own interest, no less than yours, that it should be kept, and that it will, if he communicates it, bring upon him suffering.

Let the trust be repeated, whether he violates it or not. I do not undertake to say to what extent this confidence should at first be carried; but I do feel sure that the work should in all cases be commenced, and that it would generally be successful. Perhaps the husband would at first be guilty of a betrayal or two; but he would probably soon learn better.

For my own part, I would never have many secrets which I wished to communicate. The fewer we have the better. But when we have something which we wish to communicate, it is a painful condition to be unwilling or afraid to commit it to our dearest friend. I know not what those husbands think who violate confidence, and render themselves unworthy of being trusted with a secret; but I certainly do not envy them the pleasure they feel in doing so. I should much rather be the sufferer. I should prefer, by far, to be occasionally betrayed, than never to trust. This living on guard—this standing sentry over our tongues, for fear some enemy should pass, or for fear an enemy should gain some advantage—is to be abhorred. A due degree of caution, in all we say or do, is right; and is right even in married life. But I say again, that were I a young wife, I would prefer a little suffering to that over-caution which deprives us of half that happiness without which life is scarcely worth possessing.

CHAPTER VI.

SYMPATHY.

Scripture doctrine. Miss Edgeworth's opinion. Dr. Rush's. Effects of sympathy. Disposition to vex each other. A caution. Sympathy the first step to improvement.

It is no less the command of reason than of revelation, to "rejoice with those who rejoice," and to "weep with those who weep;" or in other words, to sympathize with our fellow beings.

If, as Mrs. Edgeworth says, a being destitute of sympathy would be incapable of exercising compassion, friendship, benevolence, or any social feeling whatever, and would consequently be incapable of all intercourse with society, how deeply unfortunate must be the condition of a married couple, both of whom were in this condition! Nor would their condition be much improved, were the husband what he ought to be, while the wife remained unmoved, unsympathizing and unsocial.

Dr. Rush seems to have taken it for granted that most married people do sympathize deeply with each other; else how could he have made the conclusion—premature as we may deem it to be—that not only the habits and manners, but even the features of married people gradually approach? This certainly never would happen without the existence of deep and strong sympathy. But I think that even Dr. Rush himself must have met with many exceptions to the truth of his remark.

I suppose, indeed, that there is scarcely a being on earth who is utterly incapable of being affected more or less by others. Probably no two persons can be in each other's society for half an hour, and be active in conversation or otherwise, without *catching* something, if I may so express the idea.

Yet this sympathetic influence may not always be favorable. A person—even a wife—who should be governed by sympathy alone, would necessarily be affected by the bad as well as the good passions of others. Blindly obedient to this sentiment, she must feel resentment, anger, jealousy, and other evil passions, as well as those of a contrary kind.

But it is not this for which I am contending. A person all sympathy, or with his sympathy blinded, would be a greater evil in the world, and in particular to those about him, than one who was wholly destitute of such a feeling. I am only insisting on its due place among other affections, and especially in that relation which is the most endearing of all others merely human—the relation of husband and wife. I insist on it, too, not in any small or stinted measure, but in an eminent degree. I insist—strongly, too—that without it, matrimony would not be worth anything; while its existence would atone for the want of almost everything else.

I insist, moreover, on the necessity of cultivating this feeling, especially on the part of the wife. Everything, in this respect—or almost everything—will depend on her. If she wishes her husband to sympathize with her joys and sorrows, she must first sympathize with his. I do not say that she will always succeed to the utmost of her expectations; but I do say, as I have already said, that her efforts cannot be lost. It is not in human nature wholly to resist this influence.

Do you expect her, I shall probably be asked, to feign an interest which she does not feel? By no means. But I would have her *feel* an interest. I consider it as her duty to do so. Her marriage vows implied, or should have implied it. By her union with her husband—by becoming bone of his bone and flesh of his flesh, according to the divine intention—she *promised* to follow his destiny—to rejoice when he should rejoice, and to weep when he should weep. My only request is, that this promise be fulfilled.

In order to do this, she has but to follow nature. Were not the indications of nature opposed and thwarted by intention, I cannot help thinking that there would be, in respect to sympathy, a gradual approximation to each other, from the day of marriage to the day of death.

This may seem a strange assertion; and not a few may think it uncharitable. But I have never known an instance where there was any want of a proper sympathy between husband and wife, that did not originate chiefly in direct opposition to nature's intentions and indications.

There are persons—and some of them are wives, too—who are sure to be always opposed to those around them. If others are sorrowful or melancholy, they will, for the very reason, be the contrary. If others are grieved, they will be light or trifling; if others are under the influence of any unhappy passion whatever, they will be sure, for this very reason, to assume the opposite. They seem to do it, often, for the sake of doing it. They seem to take a diabolical delight in vexing a fellow creature; and the closer the attachment, the more will they indulge themselves in this reprehensible practice.

I have seen many wives—yes, many—who loved to vex, slightly, their husbands. I have seen a still greater number who seemed to delight in showing themselves superior to sympathy;—persons, too, who are among the first to seek the sympathy of others; and who, while they are willing to give their dearest friend mental suffering, would not, on any account, be the means, directly or indirectly, of giving pain to their bodies.

These individuals ought to consider, first, whether mental suffering is not as difficult to be borne as bodily; and secondly, whether in demanding sympathy of others, they ought not to grant it cheerfully themselves. There is a rule to be found in the greatest of books, like the following—" All things whatsoever ye would that men should do to you, do ye even so to them." I would recommend this rule to those young wives who hold their heads too high; who do not readily joy in the joys and sorrow in the sorrows of their husbands.

You will say, perhaps, you do not, and you never can view things as your husband does; and how then can you sympathize with him? I have spoken of the necessity of cultivating feelings of sympathy with him. You must enter more deeply than ever yet you have done into his feelings, plans and purposes. Such as you do not approve, you will, of course, endeavor, in an appropriate manner, to change. Should you not succeed, your labor will not be lost. You will at least have learned, more deeply than ever before, his character, and will have enlisted, unawares, your sympathies, even in what you do not like or approve.

It is in vain to hope, that your husband's efforts will enkindle that interest or sympathy of which I have been speaking; for this cannot be expected. It is most in accordance with the laws of human nature, that each should kindle the fire within for himself. At least, it is true that each for himself must first put to the wheel his own shoulder.

In speaking hereafter of the duty of making special exertion for the improvement of your husband's mind and heart, I shall have occasion once more to advert to this subject. For in no way can you lead him along the ascent which you wish, till you have first taught his heart to beat and his feelings to vibrate, as it were, with yours; and he will never, in this way, sympathize with you, till you have first sympathized with him. But when all this is accomplished—when your souls seem to be but one, and your joys and sorrows commingle, then nothing but time can limit the progress he may make, or the heights and depths to which you may carry him, in knowledge and excellence.

CHAPTER VII.

FRIENDSHIP.

Few real friends. Parents not always true friends to children. Anecdote. Stormy period of life. Necessity of a friend. Arrangement of Providence. Woman sent as the friend of man. Wives the truest friends. Four qualifications for this office. Religion considered. Enemies sometimes friends.

It is not a little strange, that those who are most interested in our welfare should often be the least successful in promoting our happiness; but so it is. The cause, however, when we once examine the case to the bottom, is quite obvious. The truth is, that our parents and other near relatives are apt, by the injudicious exercise of kindness, or rather by over-kindness, to defeat their own intentions.

So common are the instances of injury from over-kindness, that one distinguished writer asserts, as the result of extensive observation, that orphans make their way best in the world. However this may be—and I am not sure but it may be true, in regard to those whose sole object of pursuit is wealth—nothing is more certain than that they who suppose themselves our best friends, sometimes judge and practice so erroneously, as to justify the remark that our best friends are not unfrequently our worst enemies.

Few things are more to be regretted than that parents, who know most in regard to the character of their own children, should strive to palliate or conceal their faults, instead of correcting them. Let this be done by whom it may, it is not the part of true but of mistaken friendship; and in so far as it is done by the parent, that parent ought not, in strict truth, to be considered as the friend of his children.

I know this is a bold position. I know it will be startling to many to hear that parents are not always the friends of their children. But is it not true? And if true, is it not a truth that must be told? I might say that which would be still more startling. I might say that very few parents are the true friends of their children.

One of my acquaintance, a young man of much worth and of a good family, has often told me that he never knew what it was to have a friend, till he was thirty years of age. He had indeed many relatives, and they supposed themselves his friends, but he says they seldom or never acted the truly friendly part. Except in a few instances, while he was a mere child, in which he rendered himself inconvenient to his parents by his misconduct, he assures me that they seldom reminded him of his errors, or labored to improve his temper, his manners, or his habits. Especially did they avoid, as by a secret plot, telling him of any fault which would be likely to give him pain. While they should have been correcting his errors, they were praising him for his excellencies; and thus, instead of improving his character, they took the sure course to injure it.

The reason why I have gone to such an extent of illustration, in a book for young wives, will soon be seen. If parents are not the friends of their children, who will be? Even if they are what they should be, they cannot always remain so. There is a period in human life, when children cease to be controlled much by parents; and in our day, this period arrives very early. The forms of parental restraint may indeed remain, but not the reality. Boys, especially, are scarcely fourteen or fifteen years old, before they begin to think themselves too old to obey.

This feeling, I say, exists, to a greater or less extent, in the best educated families. It is connected with a peculiar state of the body and of the passions. It is the stormy period of life. It is the period in which, of all others, parental friendship is most needed, by both sexes. It is, I say, life's stormy period; and destitute, as many are, of friends in the truest sense, no wonder shipwreck is often made. The wonder is that it does not occur much more frequently.

But the danger is much greater, when those whom God intended to be our friends have never discharged that duty—when they have flattered our vanity, and palliated our errors, and taken just such a course throughout as would be approved by a decided enemy of human happiness.

Here, in this state of peril, on the sea of human life, divine Providence sends a messenger for our rescue, in the form of a female friend. If we have had friends before—if our relatives have been true friends—she is a special blessing of Heaven; but if not, she is more than any common blessing—she is an angel of mercy.

I say she is *sent*. By this I mean that such is the divine arrangement, that just at the very moment when there is a tendency in our sex to break away friendless from all restraint, and to plunge headlong perhaps into thick dangers, seen and unseen, an affection is wont to spring up in us, which holds us back, and often saves us; and which would prove, were early marriages esteemed as sacred as they ought to be, the means of saving the greater part of our sex.

Thus, then, we come to the conclusion with which I wished to begin this chapter, that woman is designed as the friend of man ; and that she alone acts up to the dignity of her sex and the intention of the great Creator, who makes it a prominent object, during her matrimonial life, to exercise true friendship for her husband.

When she has fulfilled, as she ought, this part of her mission, then she has done a great and important work. Whether friendship has never before been known, or whether it has been proffered and slighted, the result is nearly the same. She will, if wise, still prove the means, under God, of effecting a great and salutary change in the whole character. I will not say that this will always be the inevitable result ; but I am of opinion that it would usually be so. I will not say that a believing wife, who is a true friend to her unbelieving husband, would always be the means of saving his soul ; but I have no doubt that this would often be the result.

I can hardly use language strong enough to convey my sense of the importance of true friendship on the part of the young wife. The following are some of the advantages which she possesses for this exercise :

1. She has the confidence of her husband ; or at least it is fair to suppose so.

2. She has a better opportunity than any other person in the world—parents, brothers and sisters not excepted—to detect his faults, errors and follies.

3. She can better choose her time for advising him than any other person, since she is so constantly with him.

4. She is more deeply concerned in the results, since her own reputation and happiness are bound up in his; and hence her motives are stronger to discharge friendly offices.

Let nothing which I have said be construed into an approbation of marriage at an age which is wholly premature. When I speak in favor of early matrimony, I do it in view of that tendency which exists and increases in civilized life, especially in cities, to defer this subject to a very late period, which usually results in celibacy—a condition which, except in peculiar circumstances, is not only socially but morally injurious.

"Without a friend, the world is but a wilderness," says an old but true adage. But as a general rule, that person, male or female, who resolves on celibacy, resolves to be friendless; that is, destitute of the truest friends. "If you have one friend, think yourself happy," says another adage. Such a one—if you are wise in the selection—is the person you make your constant companion by marriage. And I say again, the sooner this selection is made, after we have reached the stormy period of life, the better. No matter if it be at the early age of sixteen. The union need not, and probably should not be consummated, till twenty-five; but if your hearts are united, you gain nearly all the benefits of friendship that you would if it were. Your companion elect cannot fail, if he is what he ought to be—and if not, it were better that the consummation should never take place—to act the part of true friendship, so far as circumstances may permit, and you may thus go on with the work of self-education.

There is one thing which may seem, at first view, to diminish the necessity of seeking a friend by matrimony. Admitting that our parents and other near relatives frequently, and indeed generally, fail to act the part of good and true friends, does not that giving of the heart to God which the Bible (whose authority is supposed to be acknowledged by all those for whom I am writing) enjoins, secure that object? Does it not secure to us that wisdom which cometh from above, and which cannot, of course, be *less* valuable than earthly friendship? And does it not also secure to us the true friendship of our brethren with whom we are associated?

Of the friendship of God—however indispensable and valuable—I did not intend to speak particularly in this work. But I am sorry to say, that so far as I have observed, we do not derive those advantages of true friendship from our brethren in the church which, from the nature of the relation, might be expected. That we *do not,* is indeed a great mistake. But since it is a fact, and cannot at once be wholly remedied, we must take the only course which remains. Nor can this relation ever be wholly substituted for the other, because it can never be so constant or intimate.

There is one partial substitute more. Our enemies, if we have any, are frequently our best friends, short of a matrimonial friend. They will be apt to tell us some truth. They will not scruple, it is true, to tell more than the truth, in too many instances; but this should not prevent us from reaping the benefit of the good they actually do us, in amending the faults they disclose.

The thought that our enemies are our best friends, in any case, short of the relation of husband and wife, is indeed painful; but if it be just—if the fact be so—should it be suppressed? Besides, will it not greatly enhance the general importance of matrimony? And in the present age, when there is such an obvious increase of celibacy, as well as of licentiousness, is not this a matter of the highest importance?

All this general reasoning, it may be thought, is misplaced—directed to the wrong individual. The object is, to show the importance—ay, and the necessity, too—on the part of the young wife, of being what God, in nature, and especially in the divine institution of matrimony, intended she should be. That the husband requires, more than the wife, such counsel as this, does not prove that the wife needs it not at all. Besides, the saying that he who would have friends must first be friendly, will apply here with peculiar force. The wife who wishes ardently to have her husband act the part of a true friend, must set the example. As "love, and love only, is the loan for love," so friendship only, is the loan for friendship—I mean, for a friendship which is permanent and worth possessing.

Let not the reader smile at what she may choose to call a long philosophical effort to prove the necessity of her being a friend to her husband. She may not feel its necessity, in her own case; and it may not, possibly, be needed. But for one who needs not to consider the subject—carefully, and I may say prayerfully too—there are, I am sure, a hundred who do. But if not—if the remarks of this chapter are so obviously misapplied as to impair the public confidence in the general merits of the book, such a result will so raise my estimate of human nature, that I shall not regret to see the book itself consigned to oblivion.

CHAPTER VIII.

LOVE.

Is it necessary for love to decline after marriage? Internal love increases. Means of increasing it. Doing good to others makes us love them. Anecdotes; the little girl—the deist. Love, a matter within our own control. General rule. Cautions.

It would excite a smile were I to exhort you, in so many words, to love your husbands. And yet I fear that, in too many instances, no exhortation is more needed. I fear that as society is now constituted, the love of many a young wife is very far from being what it ought to be.

There is a very general opinion abroad, that the love of husband and wife must, after marriage, necessarily begin to decline. Or if it can be kept up at all, that it can only be done by special or extraordinary exertion. This, in my view, is a great mistake.

I know there is a species of love, if it deserves the name, which declines soon after marriage; and it is no matter if it does. If there is nothing but this which attracts a young couple—if the love which has drawn them into matrimony is merely a personal, or I would rather say an external love—if the parties are neither of them bound by any mental or moral attraction, the sooner we are undeceived in a matter of such unspeakable moment, the better.

There can be no objection to external love, where it is a mere accompaniment of that which is internal. What I object to, is the making too much of it; or giving it a place in our heart which is disproportioned to its real value. Our affections should rather be based chiefly on sweetness of temper, intelligence and moral excellency. It is the internal which we should chiefly regard, and not the external, except in so far as the latter is an appropriate index of the former.

This internal love it is which will form the subject of the present chapter. It is this which I wish to have kept up and increased in the matrimonial relation. It is this to which I refer when I say, love your husbands. It is this which, instead of declining, may be made, to use language which has been appropriated to another and still more important subject, to burn brighter and brighter "unto the perfect day."

A capital mistake has been often made in regard to the means of inducing or increasing love. "It is more blessed to give than to receive," is the scripture rule ; but this has been too generally inverted, and mankind have seemed to act on the principle that it is more blessed to receive than to give.

Let me be fully understood. My paraphrase of the scripture doctrine above quoted would be the following—" We love those to whom we do good, more than we love those who do good to us;" and mankind, by their practice, seem to have inverted it. They seem to take it for granted, that we love those who do good to us more than we love those to whom we do good.

Nowhere, in practical life, is this mistake more common than in the matrimonial relation, especially in its early stages. The husband, in order to secure the affection of his companion, bestows on her a thousand little attentions and favors. He supposes that if it gratifies her to receive them, her affection will increase in proportion to their frequency, and the pleasure they seem to afford her. And the wife sometimes bestows her little attentions upon him on the same principle.

Now I do not undertake to say or intimate that such is not, in any degree, the result—for I believe quite otherwise. Indeed, we are not told that we do not love at all those who do good to us, but only that the love of the receiver is not increased by the gift in as great a degree, or rather as rapidly, as that of the giver.

This principle, fully understood, would explain to both parties why their efforts in matrimonial life to secure each other's affection and confidence, are not always proportional to their expectations. It may also prevent those feelings of disappointment which sometimes arise, and those distressing doubts whether their own confidence may not have been misplaced.

It is undoubtedly an innocent, I had almost said happy mistake, since it turns out that though we fail to secure the esteem, confidence and affection of a companion, as rapidly as we expected, we are yet increasing, unknown to ourselves, our own measure and strength of affection—perhaps as much beyond any reasonable anticipations and expectations as in the other case they fall short; so that though we are disappointed in some respects, in regard to the result of our efforts, nothing is on the whole lost. Everything we do, say, think, or even design or wish, for a companion, is increasing our own attachment to him, whatever the effect may be on his own mind and heart, in relation to us.

I am the more anxious to enforce this great principle, because, though generally assented to, it seems to me very little understood in its full extent, and still less enforced in practical life, whether in the married or single relation. **For** this purpose, you will indulge me in one or two familiar illustrations.

When I was once living, for a short time, the life almost of a hermit, there was in the neighborhood a little girl, about three years old, whose society I valued greatly, but who seemed wholly indifferent to me. To gain her attachment and allure her to my study, for the sake of that familiar conversation with little children of which I was so fond, I began to give her books, pictures, flowers, &c., as well as relate stories to her. But all, to my great surprise, to no purpose. She continued indifferent and unmoved. At last I contrived to put her upon a course of bestowing favors on me, such as flowers, fruits, and the like. No sooner was this effected, than an attachment began to spring up, as I could plainly see. And now I found her visits so often repeated that her absence would at times have been quite as agreeable as her company.

I met, one day, with a deist. He insisted that the requirement to *love our enemies* was not founded in a knowledge of human nature, since to obey it was impossible. I asked whether he was sure it was impossible. He only said he had not found it possible, by actual experiment. I asked him if he admitted the truth of the principle that doing good produces love. He replied that he did, most unhesitatingly. Then, said I, is it impossible to *do good* to our enemies? "Oh no." Now, then, I rejoined, you admit that we have it in our power to do good to our enemies, and that doing good must, from its nature, produce love to the person to whom the good is done; and yet you say it is impossible to love our enemies. He was struck with a mode of reasoning which he had not expected, and did not attempt a reply.

This is not the place to prove that when our Lord commands all his followers to love their enemies, he only means that they must love them precisely in this way—that is, by means of doing good to them; but only that, if this were all which is meant, the love of our enemies is still within our power.

This conclusion, then, that we have it in our power to love whom we will, is the grand point at which I wish to arrive, and the very point which I have introduced these illustrations to establish.

It is a conclusion, too, of the utmost importance to the newly married couple. It tells them, in the plainest language, that love need not begin to diminish as soon as the marriage ceremony is over, but that it may increase indefinitely; and that we have it in our power, to a considerable extent, to say how long it shall continue to increase, and how far it shall be carried.

If, therefore, you find there is any danger that the external attachment you have formed for your husband is beginning to decline, do not hastily conclude that there is anything wrong—anything which has been misapprehended—in forming the relation. It may be a favorable omen. It certainly will be, if its place is fully supplied by that internal attachment of which I have just now been speaking, and which is the result of doing good.

In this view, as I have already said, you have it in your power to increase the flame of internal love towards him to whom you have consented to stand as an "help-meet," and to an extent to which it is impossible to assign any limits. Wherever you are, and how great soever the attachment between you, and whether, for aught I know, in this state of existence or any other, you may calculate on an ability to increase his happiness and your own love. The secret consists in doing him good.

As to the appropriate means and methods of doing him good, it seems at first view almost unnecessary for me to say one word. And yet I am willing to do so; for there may be those who will not regard me as tedious. I shall not indeed presume to point out the particular ways and means in which a young wife can do good to her husband, but only to give a few hints. Some of these means have been set forth at full length, in preceding chapters; and others will be involved in the treatment of other topics, in chapters to follow.

One general rule may here be laid down, which is—" Do everything for your husband which your strength and a due regard to your health will admit." I will not say that it were not wise, sometimes, to go even beyond your strength—to deny yourself—and even to make a self-sacrifice. But I do insist on your going to the borders, at least, of self-denial and self-sacrifice.

Such advice, at first view, may seem to be unreasonable. It may be said that I would make woman a slave. No such thing: I would make her a christian—and a happy one. I would give her that freedom to which christianity, with its high hopes and promises, bids her to aspire.

She will not long be compelled to be a menial to her husband. He must be a brute, and worse than a brute, whom such a course of active devoted service will not arouse to corresponding action. I am not ignorant of the fact that, in some instances, the more we do for others, the more they will allow us to do for them; and that what is at first considered on all hands as gratuitous on our part, they will ere long, if continued, claim as their due.

But it is seldom thus in the matrimonial relation. Few who bear the shape, and none who have the souls of men, will permit a wife to continue long to do everything in the way I have mentioned. They will yield, and be led gradually to imbibe the same spirit. When this is done—when the husband and wife both strive to do everything in their power for each other—then will they have attained a high degree of felicity. Then, too, will they have secured, most effectually, the power to rise still higher, and to love each other more and more ardently.

It is an almost universal custom to act on the other principle—to do nothing for each other, as we pass along the road of matrimonial life, which we can help—that, like a canker, slowly eats out the life-blood of domestic happiness. Oh that husbands—but I write not now for them—oh that wives were universally wise on this subject; and that they would consider well the tendencies of these things. If I am right, there is much error abroad on this subject, and in few things is a reform more necessary.

But, it is said, we must be content to wait, with patience, for results; that we must not expect too much of the world immediately; and that woman will be elevated slowly, in the progress of things, without extra effort. It may be so. We hope it will be so. But I do not expect it, nor are expectations of this kind founded in a knowledge of human nature as it is, or as it ever has been.

CHAPTER IX.

DELICACY AND MODESTY.

Many forms of immodesty. A quotation. Modesty in matrimony. Unchaste language. Example to the husband. Specimens of bad examples.

It may be thought unnecessary to conjoin modesty with delicacy; as few of those whom this work will reach will need its counsels. A female who is wanting in modesty, it may be said, will not be likely to take up a book like this; much less to heed its contents.

This remark would be more just if the term modesty was as narrow in its application as it has sometimes been regarded—if it referred only to external or overt actions. But there is a great deal of immodesty in the world—and I fear the matrimonial relation does not always exclude it—which falls far short of overt action.

I have seen this trait of character exhibited, and with the most injurious effects, where not a word was uttered which could be directly blamed; and in some instances, where there were no words at all. I have witnessed looks which spoke as effectually as words, and which did not fail to make their natural impression on the youthful mind. I have heard the sly innuendo, and witnessed, too, the effects of that. And I have seen a wife—need I say here a mother?—who thought she would not, for the world, have been the author of either the look or the innuendo, and who yet seemed to relish both. Or at least she did not disapprove of them. But not to express disapprobation, in such cases, is always, in effect, to approve.

"I have been in families where loose insinuations and coarse innuendoes were so common, that the presence of respectable company scarcely operated as a restraint upon the unbridled tongues even of the parents! Many of these things had been repeated so often, and under such circumstances, that the children, at a very early age, perfectly understood their meaning and import."

Nothing is more deeply to be regretted than the increasingly prevalent notion, that modesty and delicacy are less necessary subsequent to than before marriage. This sentiment meets with a handsome rebuke in the "Whisper to a Married Couple." "I know not two female attractions," says the author, "so captivating to men, as delicacy and modesty. Let not the familiar intercourse which marriage produces, banish such powerful charms. On the contrary, this very familiarity should be your strongest excitement in endeavoring to preserve them; and believe me, the modesty so pleasing in the *bride* may always, in a great degree, be supported by the *wife*."

The individual who gives herself up to the use of improper or unchaste language, or even to the endurance of it unchecked, is giving up at the same time the out-posts of all human virtue. The evil of being immodest, or unchaste, or indelicate, is great enough in itself considered. But this is not all. The vices are all associated; and they who have been introduced to either, or especially to all of these, are likely soon to become acquainted with others, and perhaps the whole brotherhood of them. Let us therefore beware of an improper or indelicate word or look, or even *thought*. Let us set a guard over the thoughts; for it is out of the abundance of these that not only the mouth speaks, but the hands act. Especially is it incumbent on the wife to do this.

Every young wife may have a delicate and modest husband. But in order to this, he must first have a wife of true modesty and delicacy. She may not indeed transform him in a day, or a week; but her ultimate success, if she persevere, is certain. No husband who has the least claim to the name, can always withstand it. I know there are many husbands who are somewhat brutish; but I know, too, that there are many wives who are wanting in true delicacy of thought and feeling, and sometimes of language.

She is not truly delicate who uses, or endures patiently the use in others, of those coarse, vulgar words with which the conversation of many persons is continually interlarded; such as—"My stars!" "My soul!" "By George!" "Good heavens!" &c. Such expressions, besides being indelicate, savor not a little of profanity. They are exceedingly unbecoming in all, but especially in females.

CHAPTER X.

LOVE OF HOME.

Paul's opinion. Effects of "gadding." Anecdote. Dislike of home. Error in female education. Importance of loving home. A picture drawn by Solomon. Two pictures by Abbott. Effects of loving home on the family. Hints to the reader. The Family Monitor.

THE great apostle of the Gentiles, in his letter to Titus, has condescended to inculcate the idea that a young wife should be a keeper at home. But in order to be a keeper at home, she must first learn to love domestic life. Even Paul himself, would not have her stay at home, when she regarded it as a prison.

No small share of domestic felicity hangs on this single point. I never knew a husband very happy whose wife was fond of gadding. Taking it for granted that she rules well her own tongue while abroad—which is far from being uniformly the case—still, she cannot discharge the duties of a wife, much less those of a mother, unless she prefers home to all other places, and is only led abroad from a sense of duty, and not from choice.

The wife of a distinguished senator in Congress, from one of the New England States, assures me that for eleven years of her early matrimonial life, she never went a mile from the place of her residence. I am surprised that her husband—for he was an excellent man—should have permitted this; but so it was. She spoke of it, however, not as a privation, but as a pleasure. But there are few females, at the present day, who would do this.

On the contrary, a very large share of young wives in the fashionable world seem to tax their ingenuity to the utmost, to devise some plan for keeping away from home. One would think, by their countenance, voice and manner, that they regarded the latter as only a kind of necessary evil. And is it not so?

Where is it that the eye brightens, the smile lights up, the tongue becomes flippant, the form erect, and every motion cheerful and graceful? Is it at home? Is it in doing the work of the kitchen? Is it at the wash-tub—at the oven—darning a stocking—mending a coat—making a pudding? Is it in preparing a neat table and table cloth, with a few plain but neat dishes? Is it in covering it with some of nature's simple but choice viands? Is it in preparing the room for the reception of an absent companion? Is it in warming and lighting the apartments at evening, and waiting, with female patience, for his return from his appointed labor? Is it in greeting him with all her heart on his arrival?

Or is all this regarded—and seen by the husband to be regarded—as mere drudgery, from which she would rejoice to be exempted? Is she often found silent at home, with nobody there but her husband, heaving now and then perhaps a sigh, and uttering occasionally an anxious wish? Are her warmest expressions and sweetest tones, her happiest looks and most joyous steps reserved for the party, the concert, the call, the steamboat excursion, the lecture, the theatre or the exhibition?

It pains me excessively to know, from actual observation, that the latter is the true picture of a proportion of our modern female companions. They do not seem to marry with a view to the happiness of domestic life. They appear to regard home—the kitchen, especially—as the grave of all true freedom and enjoyment. What object such persons have in view, in entering into wedlock, it is difficult to conceive, unless it be to comply with fashion, and to avoid reproach. Do they not resemble, in some respects, the seven persons who are represented in the language of prophecy, as laying hold of the skirt of one Jew, saying—" We will eat our own bread, and wear our own apparel, only let us be called by thy name, to take away our reproach?"

There is something radically wrong in that education which permits females to come to maturity without the most exalted notions of domestic bliss, and without the highest anticipations of sharing in the honor of its creation. How much more erroneous still, to suffer them to come upon the stage of action, not only destitute of this sacred regard for domestic felicity, but even hating it. And yet I have seen many a young lady of mature years, who honestly confessed that she should dread death far less than confinement to a single house, and to the cares of a household.

How totally unfit is such a person to become a help-meet to man! How entirely disqualified to discharge the great duties which Providence assigns her in the work of educating herself and others!

If there be among my readers a young wife who has entertained these sentiments, let her consider. It is not too late. She may bring herself to take pleasure in what she now hates. Strong faith or belief in the importance of a thing, and a powerful will to execute what we believe to be right, are almost omnipotent.

Let her consider well the structure of human society. Let her consider well what is the first and most important nursery of thought and affection—the first school for the formation of human character. Let her consider who is the first—nay, the most efficient—of human teachers. Let her remember the power, as well as the influence of maternal love. Let her hearken to the voice of nature, which speaks to her of duty, and points her to the highest happiness. Let her hear the still small voice of conscience, unless that conscience has been most strangely stifled or perverted. Let her hear, lastly, the voice that speaks from heaven, which prescribes her being's end and aim, her proud prerogative, and her sacred responsibilities, and which assigns her reward.

There are no duties on earth so nearly angelic as those which devolve on woman. Let the young wife then gird herself to the work which is appointed her. Let her resolve to be what she is made to be—a messenger—an angel. Let her take hold of the promises which belong to the faithful wife, and resolve that what she knows to be her duty shall be faithfully pursued. Let her do this, and what is right will soon become agreeable, on the known principles of human nature.

We can never enough admire the simplicity and naturalness of Solomon's description of a good wife—the wise and virtuous mistress of a happy household—delighted with her home, and striving to make her husband and her maidens equally delighted and happy. The following is the portion of scripture referred to, as we find it presented in Dr. Coit's arrangement. Let not my fashionable readers, if perchance I should have any such, complain that Solomon was an old-fashioned man. If the fashions which he approves are good ones, and the home which he describes a happy one, are they less so because they were in favor three thousand years ago?

> " She seeketh wool and flax,
> And worketh diligently with her hands.
> She is like the merchants' ships;
> She bringeth her food from afar.
> She riseth also while it is yet night,
> And giveth meat to her household,
> And a portion to her maidens."
>
> " She perceiveth that her merchandize is good:
> Her candle goeth not out by night.
> She layeth her hands to the spindle,
> And her hands hold the distaff.
> She stretcheth out her hand to the poor;
> Yea, she reacheth forth her hands to the needy.
> She is not afraid of the snow for her household;
> For all her household are clothed with scarlet.
> She maketh herself coverings of tapestry;
> Her clothing is silk and purple.
> Her husband is known in the gates,
> When he sitteth among the elders of the land.
> She maketh fine linen and selleth it;
> And delivereth girdles unto the merchant.
> Strength and honor are her clothing;

> And she shall rejoice in time to come.
> She openeth her mouth with wisdom;
> And in her tongue is the law of kindness.
> She looketh well to the ways of her household,
> And eateth not the bread of idleness.
> Her children arise up and call her blessed,
> Her husband also, and he praiseth her."

This, we may be assured, was never the picture of a wife who did not love home. Nor would such a wife as this, ever have reason to complain of her husband for going abroad to seek enjoyment. Not one man in a thousand would ever absent himself, who had such a home as the virtuous woman just described presided over, during the long winter's evenings, because he was otherwise solitary. Not one in a thousand, whose habits were unvitiated, would fly from his own fireside every time he found a leisure moment, to join the club at yonder store, or the gang at the neighboring dram shop, or the motley crowd that throng the road which leads to intemperance. If all wives loved and delighted in their homes as Solomon would have them, few husbands would go down to a premature grave through the avenues of intemperance and lust, and their kindred vices.

Abbott, in his "Path of Peace," presents some very striking pictures of home. The following are selected for the sake of the contrast. The first is a home which is unhappy.

"Here is a christian lady entering her parlor in the morning. She finds that the servant has made some gross blunder in her morning duties. The breakfast table is not properly arranged; the toast, perhaps, is burnt; or tea has been provided instead of coffee. At once she is thrown off her guard. Her peace of mind is all gone. Vexed and irritated, she loads the servant with all that lady-like abuse with which not a few parlors are familiar. When the husband enters, he finds his wife with flushed cheek and clouded brow, and all the enjoyment of the morning meal is gone."

But now for the other picture.

"The husband sees his wife moving about the house serene and happy. She is faithful in the discharge of all her duties; she will not allow her feelings to be irritated by the annoyances of faithful domestics. He passes through the kitchen, and finds that the same religion which makes her cheerful in the parlor, controls her feelings there. The smile is there upon her countenance, and good nature animates her heart. My dear wife, says he, is almost an angel. Oh that I had such control over my feelings as she has over hers! Molested as she is, altogether beyond my power of endurance, by the carelessness and unfaithfulness of those whom she employs, she is still always calm, and mild, and happy.

"He comes home at night, worn down with the toil of the day, and a cheerful room and a cheerful heart embrace him. His troubled spirit is soothed by the quiet influence which she throws around him.

"Perhaps he is naturally a passionate man, and comes home vexed and petulant. But the neat fireside, the pleasant table, the peaceful home, the soothing tones of his wife's voice, calm his perturbed spirit. He feels that home is indeed a blessed retreat from the turmoil of business, and he will not leave it till duty compels him."

I do not believe one woman in a hundred has any conception of the good which divine Providence, by appointing her to be a help-meet of man, puts it in her power to do. It is not in humanity to resist, wholly, the silent influences of voice, tone, look, step, gait—everything, in one word, which constitutes example—in those whom we love. Happiness begets happiness; and domestic happiness is peculiarly prolific. He must be a brute who does not heed, feel, yield to the force of its heavenly influence, and become thereby modified, improved, adorned, exalted.

If it be asked why I do not particularize more—why I do not dwell at greater length on the methods of imparting this influence—my reply is, that it is not in the forms themselves to accomplish anything, unless there be a quickening spirit to accompany them. But if there be a spirit within—if there be a hearty desire to produce happiness ever pervading the female bosom, it will not fail to find its way forth. Not that the forms are wholly unimportant, for they are not so; but I regard their importance as only secondary.

There is, however, one condition to be complied with by every wife who would induce her husband to love home—which is, that her own cheerfulness and happiness and love, which are ever the chief instruments of human *re*formation and *trans*formation, be steady and consistent. In vain will she hope to accomplish much, who is happy by fits and starts only. Domestic bliss—whatever may be said of other bliss—is not like the agitated ocean, nor yet the perturbed stream. It does not come in the whirlwind, nor in the tornado; but in the gentle ever-fanning breeze, and in the ever-distilling dew of heaven.

I have sometimes pitied wives who have an ardent desire to render their homes and their husbands happy. Indeed, the number of such wives is larger, in this world, than our sex are sometimes wont to admit. I have pitied them, I say; but it was because neither their desires nor the accompanying efforts were uniform. Woman is not trained to give a steady light and heat like the sun, but to dazzle us, rather, with the meteor, or burn us with the comet. And until our system of female education is reversed, and woman is educated to make mankind truly happy, as a leading object, the greater part of her effort—vacillating and unsteady as it is—must be lost, as is our preaching upon her. This is not said to discourage her; for though she cannot hope to transform earth, nor even her own home, at once, into a paradise, she can do something towards it. And the less an individual can do, and the greater the necessity that the whole race should be co-workers in building up and adorning and exalting humanity, the more is it incumbent on each individual of the race to be active at his post, and to do the little in his power.

I would that women of true benevolence and piety, were not so apt to dwell on the narrowness of their sphere of usefulness, and the smallness of their means for accomplishing good. They forget, in my opinion, what doing good is. They forget, or do not know, that to make the domestic circle what it should be, is one principal object of their mission. They forget that heaven, if it begin at all, must begin below the sun; and that the fairest known type of the bliss beyond the grave, is the little world of bliss which woman forms around the domestic fireside.

The reader who wishes to dwell a moment longer on this most interesting and important topic, may peruse the following extracts from James's Family Monitor. I would only amend it by saying, that he who labors with his pen, or in the shop or factory, is no less delighted with the happy home which this writer so beautifully portrays, than he who labors in the field, under the fierce beams of the sun.

"To ensure, as far as possible, the society of her husband at his own fireside, let the wife be a 'keeper at home,' and do all in her power to render that fireside as attractive as good temper, neatness, and cheerful, affectionate conversation can make it; let her strive to make his own home the soft green on which his heart loves to repose, in the sunshine of domestic enjoyment.

"O woman! thou knowest the hour when the 'good man of the house' will return at mid-day, while the sun is bowing down the laborer with the fierceness of his beams, or at evening, when the burden and heat of the day are past;—do not let him, at such a time, when he is weary with exertion, and faint with discouragement, find, upon his coming to his habitation, that the foot which should hasten to meet him is wandering at a distance— that the soft hand which should wipe away the sweat from his brow is knocking at the door of

LOVE OF HOME.

other houses ; nor let him find a wilderness where he should enter a garden—confusion where he should see order, or filth that disgusts, where he might hope to behold neatness that delights and attracts.

"If this be the case, who can wonder that, in the anguish of disappointment, and in the bitterness of a neglected and heart-broken husband, he turns from his own door for that comfort which he wished to enjoy at home, and that society which he hoped to enjoy in his wife, and puts up with the substitutes for both which he finds in the houses of other men, or in the company of other women.

"United to be associates, then, let man and wife be as much in each other's society as possible ; and there must be something wrong in domestic life, when they need the aid of balls, routs, plays, and card parties, to relieve them from the tedium produced by home pursuits. I thank God I am a stranger to that taste which leads a man to flee from his own comfortable parlor, and the society of his wife—from the instruction and recreation contained in a well-stored library, or the evening rural walk, when the business of the day is over, to scenes of public amusement for enjoyment. To my judgment, the pleasures of home and home society, when home and home society are all that could be desired, are such as never cloy, and need no change, but from one kindred scene to another.

"I am sighing and longing, perhaps in vain, for a period when society shall be so elevated and so purified—when the love of knowledge will be so intense, and the habits of life will be so simple—when religion and morality will be so generally diffused, that men's houses will be the seat and circle of their pleasures; when, in the society of an affectionate and intelligent wife, and of well educated children, each will find his greatest earthly delight; and when it will be felt to be no more necessary to quit their own fireside for the ball room or the concert, than it is to go from the well-spread table to the public feast, to satisfy the craving of a healthy appetite. Then it will be no longer imposed upon us to prove that public amusements are improper, for they will be found unnecessary."

CHAPTER XI.

SELF-RESPECT.

A principle. Self-respect should be early cultivated. An anecdote.

EVERY person tends to become what he is taken to be; and every person is taken to be what he takes himself to be. At least, there is so much of truth in this statement that it may safely be regarded as a general rule.

Let a young lady be brought up in the belief, that she is inferior in natural capacity, to her companions of the same age and circumstances; let her, moreover, have very little respect, not only for her own natural understanding, but for her acquired talents; let her also consider herself as very low in the moral scale; let her, in short, respect herself but little—and what will be the consequence? Will she not cease to be respected by those around her, in the same proportion?

I do not say she will, in this way, wholly lose the respect of her friends; but only that she will lose a measure of it, and that this measure will be in exact proportion to the measure of her own loss of respect for herself.

In like manner, every young wife should remember that the measure of her husband's respect will be graduated by the respect she manifests for herself. If she deem it important to her happiness to appear, in his eyes, respectable, let her in the first place learn to set a proper estimate on herself, and maintain, in all circumstances, that dignity of character and that self-confidence, without which her object can never be secured.

Let me not be misunderstood. I am not encouraging pride or vanity. There is a wide distinction between these and a just self-respect. They are as unbecoming, and will as surely tarnish the lustre of your character, as the latter will add to it.

Nor am I disposed to encourage an assumption of what does not exist. Nothing will ever be gained by mere pretension. It should be your study to know what you are, and what is the measure of respect to which you are entitled, from your husband and others. And having formed a judgment, do not let your natural timidity or diffidence lead you into concessions which your judgment would not approve.

I have already treated at considerable length, on concession and submission to your husband. I have even insisted, at the risk of being regarded as *heretical*, that such concession is sometimes your duty. Yet there is no clashing in all this. Two friends of the same sex may often yield their opinions to each other, when there is danger of collision, without any sacrifice of self-respect, and without losing, in the smallest degree, the respect of each other.

I have sometimes thought that more pains ought to be taken by parents to cultivate in their children this virtue of self-respect; and I throw out the hint for the prospective benefit of my readers. I am the more disposed to do so, from the fact that I have known so many persons miserable through life, because they were wanting in respect for themselves.

M. R. was the eldest of two brothers, in a large family. The youngest was taught to respect himself; the other was made to think himself all but an idiot. The impression of his inferiority was strengthened by every possible circumstance of his treatment. And what he was taught to take himself to be, he accordingly became. With natural parts nearly equal to the average of mankind, he grew up little better or more useful than an idiot. He was, indeed, decently fitted to be a "hewer of wood and drawer of water" to some person better educated. But an independent man he never was, and never would have been, had he lived a thousand years.—This anecdote will, of course, apply to the other sex; for human nature, in this respect, is essentially the same in both man and woman.

CHAPTER XII.

PURITY OF CHARACTER.

Explanation of the term. Impurity of character very common. Case of Lucius and Emilia. Seduction. The consequences. Several hints.

THEY who suppose that less of the virtue which forms the subject of this chapter, is needed after than before marriage, have greatly mistaken the tendencies of our common nature. It is, as it were, the hinge on which everything else turns; not only in early life, but in middle age—and not only in middle age, but to the very close of our earthly existence. Nay, more than this—much more. It is one of the predominating virtues of heaven. A disposition to purify ourselves, as Christ our master is pure, is more than once, in scripture, regarded as a leading evidence of his discipleship.

But this purity of character goes much deeper than has sometimes been supposed. It is not sufficient that we abstain from open and gross misconduct at every age and in all circumstances. Nor is it sufficient that we avoid the use of words which have an acknowledged signification of this kind. I have seen those whose conduct was, thus far, for a time, unexceptionable. And all this, too, while there was ample external evidence—short of words or overt acts, it is true, but still obvious—of impurity within. It is not the "mouth," alone, nor even the mouth and the hand, that detect the "abundance of the heart."

I have seen those—and in some grades of what is even called civilized society, the instances are by no means rare—whose lives were an almost continual series of violations of every law intended to secure human purity, who yet passed among us for good and virtuous citizens.

Do you say this is a slander upon society? Would that it were so. But alas, it is too true to be regarded as slander.

Lucius and Emilia were trained as most young people are among us. They were never regarded as immoral or licentious. On the contrary, they were truly respectable, and universally beloved. Nor was there aught which was exceptionable during six long years of courtship. They were *too selfish*—were they actuated by no other motives—to stoop to anything which might, even by possibility, bring upon them the finger of public scorn or odium.

They have now been married about ten years. Alas, what a change have they undergone in their character! I do not say there is anything open and manifest, which is objectionable, but there is much within doors—seen only by the inmates of the family—which is very far from being what it should be.

I do not deny that Lucius was the first aggressor. Men, I believe, are usually the first to go astray, and the usual seducers of the other party. In the present case, this was the undoubted fact. Lucius has been acting the part of the seducer, from the very first month of matrimony.

Let not the reader smile to hear me talk of seduction after matrimony. It is scarcely less common than at an earlier period. I am speaking of seduction of mind. "The mind," says Dr. Watts, "is the standard of the man." The great evil of external impurity consists in the fact that it indicates internal impurity—an impurity of the mind and soul.

It is this impurity to which Lucius has step by step led Emilia. At first, her ear was pained by the most distant allusion which bore the stamp of licentiousness. She knew, full well, the tendency of his remarks, and they were, therefore, for a time, repulsed. But though improper remarks were forbidden, means were not wanting to seduce, which fell far short of words. And no means which promised the least degree of success were left untried.

But was it his design to injure? By no means. He never dreamed of injury; he thought only of self-gratification. He believed himself entitled, in his present state of life, to every indulgence which that state could procure, short of actual injury to the health of the parties.

It was in this view that he introduced, in the most artful manner, first his more distant allusions, then his innuendoes, and at length something bolder still. His progress was indeed slow. Day after day, for several years, brought but little change. Still a change was visible to most of the friends, especially to those who were intimate in the family.

And now that ten years have passed away, what think you is the state of things? Pitiable indeed—most truly so. Emilia is little more what she once was, than the spirit of darkness is the seraph. She is fallen. She has sunk, even in her own estimation—and much more in the estimation of others—to rise, I fear, no more. There is, therefore, seduction after marriage, as well as before—seduction of the mind and heart, I again say—and Emilia is its victim.

Do you ask what and where are the evidences? I answer—Enter the family. Watch the conduct of this once pure and happy couple. Hear that coarse innuendo. See whether it raises a blush. See whether it even induces a sorrowful look. Nay, see that oldest boy deciphering it. He has already become an adept at the business, and *his* very soul is poisoned. He is ready, on his part, when the stormy period of life shall arrive, and perhaps somewhat before that period, to become the victim of the seducer; for there are, in this lower world, seducers of males as well as of females. Ay, worse still;—he is already seduced; and—astonishing as it may appear—by his own parents. His mind and conscience are defiled, and it is of little consequence whether the motions of the body have or have not yet begun to follow the impulses of the mind and the affections of the heart.

But there is other evidence. Emilia's own personal behaviour shows traces of the destroyer. She was once as remarkable for personal neatness and cleanliness, as for modesty of speech and behaviour, and purity of heart. But both these are now rapidly disappearing, and will soon be numbered, it is to be feared, with the things that *were*. Her tongue, too, which once knew not the art of evil speaking, is now beginning to be the retailer of those petty slanders at which, twelve, and even eight years ago, she would probably have shuddered.

The path of vice is down hill; and she who has entered but one step in the path of impurity, is on the high road to everything which debases and destroys. Nor does she traverse it alone. She is sure to have company—a company innumerable—both of the fraternity of the vices and of those who personify them.

It may be said that this chapter should be directed to the young husband, or the young parent, rather than the young wife. Perhaps the suggestion is correct. And yet it seems desirable that the latter should know her danger. Prevention is my motto. "Who would not give a trifle to prevent," says an illustrious poet, "what he would give a thousand worlds to cure?"

I beg those for whom I have intended these paragraphs to ponder them well. Let them remember that their danger lies in taking first steps. Let them be guarded well at every avenue. They are often most exposed who think themselves least so. "I tremble for the man who does not tremble for himself," said a preacher on temperance; and the same might be said, with equal if not still greater force, by the preacher on purity of character. Especially is this true of him who pleads on this point with the female world.

"The character of woman," says Stanford, in the "Ladies' Gift," "is like a bed of snow; if it receive a blemish, however small and faint, it remains. Other snow may indeed fall upon it, and the frost may slightly gloss it over, but the sullied spot will still be there; and when the thaw comes, it will be discernible in the discolored mixture."

This figure is a very delicate one, but it is quite inadequate; since the small blemish upon the snow does not, of necessity, discolor the whole mass—whereas the slightest female impurity tends to extend itself till the whole character is affected by it. Nor does its influence end here; it moves on, affecting multitudes by example, and propagating itself, like the divided polypus, to infinity.

CHAPTER XIII.

SIMPLICITY.

Simplicity a virtue. Very rare. Simplicity of language.- Story of Mrs. L. Simplicity of conduct.

WHEN I say that I consider simplicity a virtue in a young wife, I mean not by the term weakness of intellect, or any want of common sagacity. But I mean, rather, great plainness of language, dress and manners—an entire artlessness and freedom from everything which savors in the smallest degree of cunning or duplicity.

This simplicity is an ornament of great price in any individual; but it is especially becoming in the young married lady. It is one, moreover, which she should watch over, and be exceedingly studious to preserve.

The necessity of preserving and cultivating simplicity of character, is enhanced by the consideration that, like other gems, it is exceedingly rare among us, and is every day becoming more so. The young wife, whether she comes from the family or the boarding school, is very apt to bring with her almost anything else, rather than this trait; and as she is now to commence an era in her life, it seems highly desirable that she should commence right. Hence it is, that I press upon her attention a due regard to simplicity.

She should study simplicity in dress. But on this point I need not enlarge, as I shall have occasion to recur to it hereafter.

She should study great plainness of speech. She should say just what she thinks. I do not, indeed, undertake to show that she should say *all* she thinks; for that were quite another matter. Only let what is said, be exactly what is thought, and intended, and felt.

Nothing can be more foolish, than anything like art or duplicity in the LANGUAGE of a wife to her husband. I know that some husbands like it well enough at first; but it is because they do not discover its tendency. They at length become sick of it themselves; and will, if it be continued, despise her for it.

Let me urge this point the more, from the fact that to be simple requires great self-denial. Everywhere in society this virtue is becoming old-fashioned and vulgar. You will need, therefore, to be armed for battle; otherwise you will surely be swept along in the full tide of a wretched and despicable fashion, till your end is destruction—I mean, morally so.

Do not be afraid of being laughed at. Mrs. L., an individual with whom I was formerly acquainted, was bred to be artless and sincere. She was just what she seemed to be. When she said a thing, you would know she spoke her heart. It would not require to be, like a foreign language, translated. If she approved of this or that statement, or of this or that course of conduct, you would know she did in sincerity. If she disapproved, you would know she was still equally artless and sincere.

True, she did not pass her judgment on everything said and done around her in the world. She knew that it was very difficult to know all the various motives by which mankind are actuated and governed, or to understand all the circumstances of an action, after it is brought forth. She was therefore slow to decide on merit or demerit. But whenever she felt herself really called upon to speak or give an opinion, she gave it in sincerity. She meant exactly what she said. True, she was modest in her remarks; and when forced to dissent from the opinion of those around her, or to say that which she thought would be likely to give pain, she did it in the kindest possible manner.

And what was the result of this simplicity? Did it secure the confidence and friendship of those around her? Or did it excite their ridicule, or awaken their displeasure?

I am glad to have it in my power to state, that it not only secured the friendship of most of those who knew her, but it always enabled her to retain the friends she had once acquired. Especially did it secure the full confidence of her husband. He knew exactly where to find her; he knew, therefore, how to prize her.

A few indeed laughed, and called her silly. But who were they? The butterflies that, though they appear so gay and promising in the morning, have half flitted out their days at noon? The busy, heartless throng, that meet to say—" How do you do?" and " How glad I am to see you!" and " How I hoped to have seen you long since, at my room!" and " You must call as soon as possible, or I shall never forgive you;" and yet care not one straw about you, after all these pretensions? Yes, these were the persons who laughed. The sober, sensible part of the community have something else to do besides laughing at good sense. They rejoice at it as a pearl of great price, wherever they find it.

But duplicity of CONDUCT, however common among us, is equally despicable with duplicity of language. Indeed, they commonly exist together, like twin sisters; and are not more easily separated. Avoid both as you would the breath of the pestilence. Cultivate simplicity, in the fear of the Lord, with all the earnestness required by an apostle of old, in his letters to Timothy. In short, if you would go through the world happily, and reach the bar of an approving God, strive with all your power, not only to be what you ought to be, but to be what you seem to be.

CHAPTER XIV.

NEATNESS.

Great importance of neatness. Want of it. Effects on the husband. Neatness in small matters. Structure of the skin. Necessity of bathing. Effect of neatness on morals. Effect of example. Difficulties considered. How to train a husband to slovenliness. Want of neatness in little things.

NEXT to purity of character, one of the most important duties of the young wife is, personal neatness. It is, indeed, a duty to herself, independently of her husband, since it has much to do with her own physical comfort, health and happiness.

The eccentric Cobbett has inveighed loudly against a want of personal neatness in the female sex. I will not here imitate him; but if the heat of his temper had never led him to express himself, not only forcibly but vulgarly on any other topic than this, he might well be pardoned. For next to impurity, I say again, few things are more reprehensible in a female than slovenliness.

I know well that some husbands *appear* to retain their first affection for their wives, even after they find them wanting in neatness. But because such things sometimes happen, will you run the risk? A husband may consider that the fault is in part his own. In other words, he may consider, when he finds you deficient in neatness, that he ought to have known it earlier; and that since he did not, it would be wrong in him to let this circumstance prove a source of matrimonial misery. He may therefore be silent about what he would gladly prevent; since silence is, in such a case, the only course of wisdom. But it is not possible, in such a case, for the affection of a husband to increase, or even to continue; and she is unwise who calculates upon it.

What has been said thus far, on the subject of neatness, is intended to apply to those points of human conduct which come under general observation. But there are a great many things that escape the public eye, which must not be overlooked, and which, with a person as nearly related as the husband is to the wife, cannot fail to have an influence.

The world around you can indeed discover an uncleanly face or hand, as well as your husband. But the world do not always discover so readily an uncleanly skin in general. And yet there are not a few who pride themselves on the neatness of the tips of their fingers and the most prominent parts of the face—nay, who even wash to their wrists, and their ears, and quite beyond their ears, to their shoulders—who suffer their feet and the rest of their skin to remain unwashed for weeks or months; and I am afraid sometimes nearly the whole year round.

Perhaps these persons do not always know the nature and structure of the human skin. Perhaps they do not know that there is not only a dense fog escaping from the surface of the body, at all points, during our whole existence, if we are in health, but also a continual oozing out of an oily substance on the surface of the skin, which, together with the moisture and the dust which reaches us through our clothes, constantly renders our person more or less unclean. I suppose, indeed, that such is the ignorance of most persons, of the human economy, that even this very plain and common fact, may have eluded their observation and escaped their attention.

But let those who read these paragraphs, if they have hitherto remained in ignorance on this subject, resolve to look into the matter. At the present day, and in a young wife, such ignorance is unnecessary; nay, it is sometimes unjustifiable. There are books enough accessible to every person, which teach this simple doctrine of the human economy; and she who makes the least pretension to duty and responsibility as a wife, should not delay to acquire this species of knowledge.

I have sometimes thought common sense might teach any female of real delicacy, that she ought to wash herself effectually to her wrists and shoulders, at least every day. Nay, even further; one might almost believe that the odor of our bodies—so soon changed by remaining dirty—would remind us of the necessity of a general washing equally often. But it is not so. So far from it, indeed, are some of our young people, that they actually laugh at the promulgation of such an opinion, by the accomplished authoress of the "Young Lady's Friend."

From the young wife, however, better things are to be expected. It is hoped she will investigate the whole subject for herself, and govern her conduct according to the judgment she is led to form. Should her investigations be anything worthy of the name, I shall be satisfied; since I believe they must result in a conviction of the truth of the doctrines I am attempting to promulgate.

The conclusion, then, to which I have arrived, in the progress of my own observations, and reflections, and investigations, is, that no person of either sex, be the employments followed ever so much within doors and exempt from dust, can safely neglect washing the whole body effectually once a day, both in winter and summer. I say safely; because the neglect referred to is incompatible with health.

But this is not all. It is not the mere health of the body that is concerned. Somehow or other, there is a very close connection between the purity of the body and that of the mind. And however slow or unwilling certain individuals among us may be to admit this connection, it is not the less true that it exists. The purity of which I have spoken at considerable length, in a former chapter, will hence be much more easily preserved, while the love, and confidence, and affection of the husband, if he be a man of sense, will be confirmed and strengthened.

Besides these considerations, her example, if known, will greatly affect her husband; and if he be a busy man—a New Englander—there is little doubt that he will need—and greatly, too—the silent influence of her example. Nor will he be the only individual who, in the common course of things, will be thus affected. Habituated to daily and thorough ablution, the use, and pleasure even, of the exercise, will be often discoursed upon in the family; and it is highly probable, to say the least, that she will, without exception, be imitated.

I shall unquestionably be reminded here—rather should be, were I to meet the reader face to face—

of the difficulties of daily ablution. "We have no means for heating water, nor any bathing tubs. You would not surely require us to plunge into the sea or the river."

No; I would not *require*, peremptorily, anything. If there were opportunities for sufficient retirement, I should have no sort of objection to either, during the summer. To the cold of the sea or the river, I should not certainly object; provided you were in good and vigorous health.

But there is no necessity for exposure of this kind. Nor is there any absolute need of bathing tubs. They are convenient, it is acknowledged—but not indispensable. Nor is warm water indispensable. No person, of tolerable vigor, who will begin the practice in June, July or August, need fear to wash his whole body once a day in water of the common temperature of the atmosphere. And any one who will commence in either of those months, and persevere in the practice, will find no difficulty in continuing it through the winter, and even through her whole life.

It has been said that bathing tubs are not absolutely indispensable. Many a person who washes daily, uses nothing but a common wash bowl. A quart of water, with those who have hands and know how to use them, will accomplish the object. Then, after washing, a coarse towel is needed;

and it is exceedingly useful to follow the wiping of the body with the towel, by friction. This may be done with a dry towel, or with the naked hand, or with coarse mittens, or, if you prefer it, with the flesh brush.

But neatness in our apartments is little less important than neatness of person. I hardly need remind sensible women of the importance of using as well as possessing the broom and duster; and yet there are individuals who need to be thus reminded. Some husbands have eyes as well as women; and though they may become by degrees accustomed to almost anything, you are in danger of going too fast, and at once disgusting them. If you are really determined to let your broom and duster go without being used, unless it be when some friend or other visitor is announced, you ought to be exceedingly slow in bringing about the change, for fear of the disgust of which I have already spoken. I have seen men who appeared to retain their affection for their slovenly wives; but the latter had been careful not to initiate them into the mysteries of slovenliness too soon after marriage.

A certain young man of the utmost external neatness, was united for life to a young woman of habits equally neat, at least apparently so; and yet three years had not elapsed before their dwelling exhibited, both externally and internally, the most unequivocal signs of disorder, confusion and slovenliness. How was the change effected? Simply by slow and cautious management. Taking advantage of a blind affection and an almost unreasonable partiality, she had gradually thrown her chains round him, and made him not only a slave, but a willing one.

She who means to train her husband to the same want of neatness in person, dress and apartments, in which she herself loves to indulge, should also avoid brushing down the cobwebs, which attach to the sides of the room. I have seen cobwebs hang about the corners and ceiling of rooms, which were under the care of those who were not by any means noted for slovenliness, for months together.

This may be the proper place for adverting to certain other habits, which are a violation of that general neatness and delicacy which, somehow or other, appear to have a sort of relation to the internal character. I allude to a class of habits, gained, in all probability, at the infant or district school—while there compelled to sit motionless, contrary to nature—and not broken up, either in the boarding school or the family; and which I should feel a good degree of reluctance to name, were it not that I have seen some young husbands disgusted with them. Such are the habits of rubbing the eyes, or handling the ears or the nose, or scratching the head or other parts of the body.

These habits, if pardonable elsewhere, and by every other person, will not be so by the young husband, unless he is half a brute; at least, if it be long continued. I repeat the sentiment. She who continues these little habits—small as they seem to be—will be much more likely to suffer, in her husband's estimation, than she who commits many other errors, in themselves of far greater magnitude. These stand out so prominent, that they make their full impression; and the impression is distinct and lasting.

But if these smaller habits are so bad, what shall I say of snuff-taking, and its consequences? What shall I say, especially, of snuff-taking in a lady who is cooking for the family? But a word to the wise should be sufficient, and here I leave the subject, only regretting the painful necessity I felt of introducing it.

CHAPTER XV.

ORDER AND METHOD.

Order, heaven's first law. Importance to the house-keeper. Book-learning. Prejudices against it. Story of Fidelia. Consequences of disorder.

"Let all things be done decently and in order," is the injunction of an inspired penman; and a highly distinguished poet has pronounced order to be the "first law" of Heaven. But however it may be in the economy of heaven, of one thing we may be certain, which is, that it is exceedingly important on earth. There is no employment whatever—be it ever so trifling—in which it is not of the first importance to preserve a due degree of order.

But valuable as order is, it is nowhere more so than to the house-keeper. She who has no regular method of doing things, and who observes no order in her proceedings, will accomplish very little, in comparison with those who are more orderly.

Every one indeed has some method of doing things, whenever they are performed; but the number of those who do things in an orderly manner is, I fear, rather small. I am led to think it is so, from observation. I see industrious, hard-working women, toiling like slaves all day long, to perform an amount of labor that I am fully persuaded many others, of no greater strength, would perform equally well in half the time. I say I see this, not *occasionally*, but often. I see it, in fact, everywhere; but especially in the houses of the middling and the poor.

Mrs. Child's "Frugal Housewife," with a portion of our American community, has probably had a salutary influence, in this respect. There are those who are willing to cultivate order and method in housewifery. They are willing to do it merely for their own convenience. They are willing to do it for the sake of economy. They are willing to do it, moreover, for the sake of their husbands. I rejoice that the number of such persons is greatly increasing; and that the army of those who choose to remain in ignorance is rapidly diminishing.

Still there are those who are as yet held in chains by prejudice. They do not believe in this book-learning, as an aid to housewifery, they tell us; and so they shut up the avenues to improvement from that source. Others, still more numerous, suppose their own methods are the best which can be devised; and only pronounce others excellent, in proportion as they conform to or resemble their own.

As to order, a large portion of our community seem to me to have no order at all, except *dis*order. Nor will they be persuaded to any other. We may lay it down here as a general rule, that they who do business most at hap-hazard, and with the least regard to order, will be found to have imbibed the strongest prejudices against it, and to be least favorably disposed towards method and order both.

Fidelia is a young wife of a different description. She has a small family to take care of, consisting of her husband, herself, a hired man, and two small children. She forms her plan, in part, the preceding evening—but it is only in part. At five o'clock in the morning, she is up, planning her work for the day, which usually takes up a considerable time. But it is all planned; there is no mistake about it. There is a place, in her plan, for every kind of business which can possibly come up during the day; and everything is done at its time and in its place. By rising early, she gets before her business; and then it is not at all difficult for her to keep before it all day. She has time even for occasional interruptions, should they happen.

Those who will neither form their plans during the previous evening, nor rise early to do it in the

ORDER AND METHOD.

morning, must continue to suffer the consequences. Happy would it be if none but themselves were sufferers. Happy would be the condition of some husbands, could they escape the disorder produced by disorderly wives, and breathe freely once more their native element.

CHAPTER XVI.

PUNCTUALITY.

Punctuality lengthens life—is indispensable. Its influence on others. Various forms of punctuality. Anecdote. Reflections. Case of the farmer. The wife's excuses. Real state of the case. Appeal to those whom it concerns.

ONE of the more important of the common duties of a wife is punctuality. To so great an extent does her own happiness, as well as that of her husband, depend upon it, that I have sometimes wondered how any woman of good sense could overlook it. Yet nothing is more common.

It is almost in vain that you regard method and order, if you disregard punctuality. You may plan ever so well—you may have everything properly arranged, so far as mere theory is concerned, in the very best manner—you may even perform everything, when you do once attend to it, in the best possible manner;—and yet if a want of punctuality be a predominating trait in your character, you will wear away much of life to little purpose. It is verily believed that the lives—the *real* lives— of people, vary in length, where years are equal, from one fourth to one third of the period commonly allotted.

Besides, were there no actual loss to the housekeeper herself, there is great loss to those around her. They catch her example. They lose by her delay. Their tempers are disturbed by her mismanagement. This last remark is especially applicable to the husband. Many a young husband has been greatly discouraged by his wife's want of punctuality; and some have been completely ruined.

There are various forms in which this defect of character appears. One of its prominent forms, in a young house-keeper, is in regard to the preparation of meals. This subject may be illustrated by the following example, rewritten from another work of the author. It is the story, or rather the complaint, of a young husband about his wife; and may afford to many a person a valuable hint.

My companion, says the complainant, is one of the best women in the world, except in one single thing—she is wanting in punctuality. In this point, in relation to everything, she utterly fails. If there be an appointment—a specified hour—no matter for what purpose, whether for rising, meals, rest, performing a job of work, calling on a friend, or even attending to religious duties or services—she is never ready at the time. She hurries and frets and vacillates, and yet she is always too late, do what she will. Now, excellent as is her character in all other respects, and invaluable as she is as a companion, as a friend, and even as a housekeeper, this single thing—this single point of failure—embitters all my happiness, and greatly diminishes her own.

I am most troubled by her want of punctuality in regard to meals—breakfast, in particular. I am a sort of literary man. I am in the habit of rising at five o'clock throughout the year. My wife lies much later; and we do not pretend to have breakfast till eight o'clock. The lateness of the hour occasions very little inconvenience. I know indeed that it is better to take breakfast soon after we rise; but habit will soon accustom us to wait three hours, without any immediate inconvenience, and perhaps without any considerable degree of suffering which is more remote.

The precise time of breakfasting, I say, then, I care very little about, provided I can have a set time, and not depart from it. But herein consists the trouble of which I was going to speak.

Though I have told my wife, perhaps a hundred times, how the matter is—though I have given her, again and again, every reason why it is indispensable, in my business, that breakfast should be ready precisely at the time, and though it is now nearly nine years since I have been laboring to get things right in this respect, I do not see but I am just as far from having attained my object as I was nine years ago.

I have told her, always, that I had no very strong objection to having breakfast ready at a few minutes before the time, but it ought never to be a minute later. I have told her of the advantages she herself would derive from forming a habit of punctuality, and that I thought she might as well begin with being punctual in regard to breakfast as in anything else.

She understands, fully, my reasons, and the weight of my arguments, and sometimes makes promises—sincere ones, too, I have no doubt—of reformation. Perhaps she succeeds in keeping her promise for a day or two—I believe she has done so once; but such is the tyranny of habit, that she soon slides into the old track again—and instead of having breakfast upon the table at eight, it does not arrive till three, five, ten, and sometimes nearly fifteen minutes afterward.

What grieves me most is, that my poor wife herself suffers a great deal on my account, although her suffering—like many other sufferings from sin—does not tend at all to her reformation. She goes on just as before. She is up late, has the tea on the table late, and everything late. At last, before she hardly thinks of it, and before breakfast is half ready, she perceives that it is within a few minutes of eight o'clock.

As soon as she perceives that the clock is about to strike eight, she begins to fret and hurry herself, and all others concerned ; and in flying from place to place to get just so many plates, and cups, and saucers, and knives, and forks, and spoons, she not only knocks down chairs, and perhaps breaks one or two, but throws down one or two of the children, who immediately set up an outcry, which renders the "confusion worse confounded" than before. Moreover, she gets so much excited, not to say fatigued, in the scrape, that she loses half the comfort of her own breakfast.

How many times have I told her, that if she could not get breakfast ready at eight without so much trouble, I was quite willing she should fix the hour at half past eight, or even at nine. But no, that will not do, she thinks. Half past eight, or especially nine, would be an unfashionable hour; and what would people say about it?

I do not suppose, by the way, that it would mend the matter at all, if the hour was put a little later; for if it were at nine, or even at ten, she would probably—such are her nature and habits—be just about as much later than the time appointed as she now is.

I have lately tried a new plan. We confine ourselves almost entirely to bread for our morning meal; or at least to a single article—as bread, or rice, or potatoes. We do it partly, indeed, from principle—because we believe it to be best; but partly, too, in order to lighten the task of my poor wife, and enable her to be punctual about getting ready the breakfast. One set of plates, and a single set of knives and forks, are all the furniture which our plain arrangements require. At least, this is the plan which we have pursued for the last six months. And as we are temperance folks, and drink nothing but water at our meals, this saves the trouble of " boiling the tea-kettle," or making either tea or coffee.

I have also, again and again, offered to hire a girl—much as I hate the practice of having domestics in the family; but my wife says—and I think justly—that it would not mend the matter at all, if I should; and that a girl would hinder her just about as much as she would help her. I have offered to confine myself to a single article—a piece of bread, or some bread and milk, or anything else—anything, in short, to secure punctuality— but all to no purpose. And now, sir, what is to be done?

A frightful exhibition this, reader, of the evils which flow from a want of punctuality. But this is only a single case, or rather a part of a case. Here is only a single person perplexed and compelled to lose time. I have seen the evil greater—at least it was more sensibly felt—among our farmers and mechanics, than anywhere else.

I have seen, many a time, a farmer with his six or eight or ten or twelve hired laborers, or a master mechanic with a large number of journeymen and apprentices, made to wait five, ten or fifteen minutes for their dinner, when they were in a prodigious hurry, and grudged every moment of the time they were obliged to wait. How must the young wife of the employer feel, in such circumstances? Does she not know the vexation of her husband? He was to come at half past twelve, with his workmen, and she knew it. Why then is not the dinner in readiness? It ought to be.

She will say that the pot would not boil, or she was absent a few moments, and the fire went down, or she mistook the time; or she will make some other equally frivolous excuse. The truth is, she puts off everything till the very last moment, as do nearly all people who are wanting in punctuality. They will not start for church, when it begins at ten, till the clock strikes—and then perhaps all is hurry and confusion of mind, no less than of body, till they get there; nor are they then fit for the services, such of them as remain. They will not send their children to school, till the hour has actually arrived when they ought to be there.

The truth is, after all, that these persons who are so wanting in punctuality, are either wanting in one thing more, viz., conscientiousness, or else they are not yet really convinced of their error. To those who are wanting in conscientiousness, I have nothing to say; for I should despair of doing them much service. They will say, yes, and promise reformation; and yet go their way and forget what manner of persons they are, and what promises they have made of reformation.

But to those who are not yet fully convinced of the importance of punctuality, and who regard the individual who insists on it as a cardinal virtue, to be a man of whims, or a dealer in little things, I would put the following questions.

Have you properly considered how easy a thing it is to be punctual, if you really desire to be? Suppose you are to meet another person at twelve o'clock, is there any difficulty in being on the spot five or ten minutes before the time? Nelson was on the spot always fifteen minutes before the time; are your moments more valuable than his? If the school commences at nine, is there any serious difficulty of having your children there at the time? If breakfast is to be at eight, is there any difficulty in the way of having it ready five minutes before the time? Your plan is to have it ready at eight, but you are too late by only five to fifteen minutes; —you always have it ready by that time. Why not fix the hour at a quarter past eight, and then it would always be ready at that time; or if it were ready a little sooner, you might wait till that time, unless all the company should chance to be present. Or if eight must still be the hour for sitting down, why not form your own plan to have all ready at a quarter before eight?—and then, of course, it would be ready at *eight*. Or are you so enslaved to hot food, as to prefer to go without your meal rather than run the risk of having it stand till it gets a little cool?

Do you know how much is the value of the time of ten men, who are compelled by your tardiness to wait ten minutes each for their dinner? Here are a hundred minutes of valuable time lost to them; how much is that a month?—how much a year? I say nothing of the vexation, but only the pecuniary loss.

If any persons who have read the foregoing remarks still think that I lay too great stress on little matters, I only wish they may be led to take a fair and impartial view of the matter, and of the consequences that, everywhere in society, flow from a neglect of punctuality; not in the mere matter of eating, &c., but in all the ordinary concerns of social and domestic life.

CHAPTER XVII.

EARLY RISING.

The young wife should rise early. Means of forming the habit. Retire early—with a quiet stomach—a quiet mind. Resolve strongly. Early training. Mr. and Mrs. Clifford. Samuel Sidney. Reflections.

THE young wife should be an early riser. Early rising is, indeed, a prominent duty of all; but it is especially incumbent on those who influence, direct, and control a family—even if that family consist of no more than the wife and her husband. For it sometimes happens that the husband needs the example of his wife to rouse him. There are those who never learn this important habit till they learn it of their wives; and wo be to those who lose, by the indolence of the latter, this only remaining chance of reformation.

I trust I need not dwell, here, on the importance of early rising, in the abstract. This matter, as it appears to me, has been treated with sufficient ability and minuteness elsewhere. I know not how any person can resist the united arguments in favor of the practice. I know not how a conscientious person—especially a christian—can continue to lie in bed late in the morning, when he knows perfectly well that it is injurious to his health, that it involves an actual loss of pleasure, and a great waste of time and property.

But how shall one who has been trained otherwise acquire this invaluable habit?

1. She should retire early the previous night. Whatever number of hours she allots herself— whether six, seven or eight—let her by all means be in bed and asleep soon enough to give her that number of hours for actual sleep, before the arrival of the period at which she proposes to rise. If she proposes to rise at four o'clock, and believes she needs seven hours for sleep, let her be sure of being in bed so much before nine as to be sound asleep by that hour.

There are many, who, in the last mentioned circumstances, would never think of going to bed till the clock had actually struck nine. Then something remains to be done, and perhaps is done in a hurry; and it is doubtful whether the individual gets to bed before half past nine, or to sleep before ten. Now this will never do. No person will, in this way, ever acquire the habit of rising at his appointed early hour. That *order* and *method* which I have recommended in a preceding chapter, must come in here, to prevent any such delay or protraction of the evening labors as shall stand in the way of going to bed quietly at the proper time.

2. She should retire with a quiet stomach and nervous system. She must not think to eat a hearty supper, one, or two, or even three hours before she retires; for though a meal of wholesome and proper food may be digested, and the stomach emptied, in three hours in the morning, it may not be so in the evening, when we are fatigued. She must not only avoid a late hearty supper, but she ought indeed to avoid taking anything whatever, unless it be water, for at least two or three hours before retiring. The person who retires by nine, should not take supper later than six. She should especially avoid, at this hour, things which are indigestible, or otherwise improper.

The observance of this last rule may exclude her, if she lives in the city, from convivial parties in the evening, which begin at a late hour. Now there is no sort of objection to having a few neighbors meet in the evening, for social conversation or other purposes, provided they do not continue so late that it interferes with their usual hour of retiring;—on the contrary, I think it may be highly conducive to health and happiness. But the growing custom of our cities—and I fear the custom is extending beyond the city—of having large parties which do not commence before eight or nine o'clock, and which include oysters, or "tongues," or wine, or all these and many more abominations, is one that should not be so much as named in a community of people calling themselves christians; even if it be encouraged—as I hear it is in some instances—by those who have reputation and influence.*

3. She should retire with a quiet mind. Now the convivial parties, and the refreshments—so called—which they furnish, and the state of the nervous system and brain which they induce, have most undoubtedly a powerful agency in producing mental inquietude, or at least in discomposing and disturbing the mind. The very excitement of a large company, if nothing improper is taken into the stomach, will do this. But when food is taken at this late hour, and after a previous evening meal, and when wine, and above all, those common narcotic medicines, tea and coffee, are used,

---

* I know what is the common defence of these enormities. I know we are told how fully employed people are during the day, and how seldom they would associate were it not for this custom. But they have no right, as christians, to be thus constantly employed, in the first place; and in the second place, the practice defeats its own object, by seeming to give people full license to keep aloof from each other at all other times. There are no greater real strangers to each other than those who attend fashionable parties.

the mental excitement, and consequent mental inquietude, are greatly increased.

There may, however, be an excited mind from causes independent of all these. There may be cares of the family, or cares of some other kind, which are preying upon the brain and nervous system, and which, if they permit sleep, do not permit that which is truly quiet, sound and refreshing. It is disturbed by dreams; or, still worse, it is broken by nightmare, or by nervous twitchings or spasms; and we rise unrefreshed and unhappy.

Nothing is more common than for people to rise in the morning with bad feelings in the head or stomach, or with a bad taste in the mouth. And yet nothing is more certain than that whenever this does happen, there has been some dietetic error—something wrong in eating or drinking, or both. The causes may, indeed, in part, lie a great way back, in errors which were at least *begun* months or years before; and which it may take months and years of a correct course to cure. But error there must have been, I say again, somewhere.

4. The young mistress of a family, who desires not only to do her own duty thoroughly to God and her fellow men, but to set a worthy example to her family, and to begin that example betimes, must not only attend to all the suggestions of the

preceding paragraphs, but she must go to bed with a strong determination to awake early, and with confidence that she shall do so. She must almost, in this respect, hope against hope. And when the morning—her hour of the morning—comes, she must not indulge herself in another moment of sleep. The plea of the sluggard—a *little* longer—must not be so much as made or thought of. No matter how poorly you have slept—unless in extraordinary cases of disturbance by fire, accident, sickness, &c.—nor how your head feels, nor how badly your mouth tastes; quit the bed instantly. The truth is, that this lying and dozing, which so many people crave and allow themselves in the morning, does not cure the bad taste of the mouth, or the bad feelings of the head; or if it does, it does not prevent their future recurrence. No, you must bound out of bed instantaneously, as soon as you have the least consciousness of your situation.

These last suggestions are of indispensable importance. No person who has not been trained to early rising from the first, will ever become an early riser—and yet rise cheerfully—without going to bed with a strong determination to spring up at the instant of waking. Nor must she be satisfied with repeating this once, or twice, or a dozen times. It must be persevered in till it becomes habitual.

Happy indeed is she who has been trained to early rising from her infancy; who has never known, in this respect, the bitterness of repentance, or the trouble of reformation. Still there is a pleasure to be obtained by rising above the contrary habit, of which the sluggard never dreamed.

Serena was always a late riser. She was trained to late rising. Do you ask if she was taught it directly? Oh, no. By example then? No. Example and precept were otherwise. But she was, in her early life, always *called* up, arbitrarily. No motives were set before her for self-exertion; no reasons for making her own will cooperate with the will of her parents. "Serena, get up," was all that was ever said, except that if she did not get up she was scolded. Now there is no surer way than this, that I know of, for infixing in the minds and feelings of mankind, a dread of early rising; and yet, is it not very common? And is not the frequency of calling up daughters, one reason why a greater proportion of them than of sons are late risers?

Mr. and Mrs. Clifford are perfect antipodes of each other, as to rising in the morning. Mr. C. is always up long before daylight. For forty years he has gone to bed almost as soon as the fowls, and risen long before them. His wife, on the contrary, late to bed, is always late to get up. Mr. C. is always calling her, and always fretting at her delay. He calls the children too from day to day, year after year; but they, encouraged perhaps by the mother, delay in the same manner.

He plans the business of the day early, and wishes early to begin it. Sometimes he tells Mrs. C. how it is the night beforehand, and says—" Now to-morrow morning you *must* be up early." She half consents to do so. But she rose late, and instead of being *before her business*, that has been before her and pressing her all day, and at nine o'clock is still unfinished; and from nine to ten is often the busiest part of the day. At ten, perhaps, or a quarter past, she gets to bed. But she tosses about with a half-crazed brain till eleven and sometimes till twelve; and when she is called at five, she only half wakes, and "feels so bad" that she must lie a *little* longer. Well, here she is, half sleeping and dozing till six o'clock, when she again rises, feeling more miserable than she did at five, and more disposed to fret and to retort the charges which her husband brings against her.

I do not know a family made more miserable by a single bad habit, unless it be in the case of one or two drunken husbands, than is the family above mentioned, by the mother's late rising.

In the first place she makes herself miserable. She is not unfrequently found repenting most bitterly of her error. But then she never seems to exercise a strong will—the first step towards curing it. Besides the bitterness of a kind of half repentance, she is always in a fret. By rising late, as I have before hinted, she gets behind her business, and is driven and harassed by it the whole day.

In the second place, she makes her husband extremely miserable, and always has done so. His plans, if he forms any, are often broken up, and he feels that he loses the best part of the day, and of life. You will say, Why does he not go to work before breakfast? He is a farmer, and a part of his fields lie at the distance of a mile from his house; and it would be very inconvenient to do so.

In the third place, this perpetual quarrel, as I might call it, has had a very bad influence upon a large family of children. Not only are they nearly all late risers, but they are fretful, peevish and bad tempered. In short, to repeat what I have already said, it is a miserable family.

Could every young wife have before her mind a correct picture of Mr. Clifford's family, as it now is, and be able to trace the effects so visible in it, to their causes, as I am, few, it seems to me, would hesitate to make the resolution to become, at all hazards, early risers. They would not think of evading the claims, in this respect, of a husband and family. They would not only regard early rising as an indispensable duty to them, but as a duty to God.

Samuel Sidney is a thriving young farmer on the Green Mountains of New England; but I would not give much for thrift obtained at such a sacrifice —the sacrifice of peace, domestic happiness and a good temper.

When he was first married, he was extremely poor, and obliged to labor by the day for support. As his most usual employers lived at a distance, and as they expected moreover that he would breakfast at home, he used to urge his wife to rise and get breakfast seasonably. It was in vain that he told her of the importance of being at work early—that his employer sometimes even complained of his coming late, &c. She would promise to rise "to-morrow morning" in good season, if he would only awake her. Well, she was awaked at the appointed time, and an effort was made to rise. But the effort was feeble, and as the call was not immediately repeated, she soon began to doze again. Sometimes her husband used to awake her two or three times before he could get her up. In short, the breakfast was late, after every effort; and the husband lost, usually, from one and a half to two and a half hours of the best of the day for labor, besides trying exceedingly the patience of his employer.

I used sometimes to wonder why he did not get his breakfast himself, as I once knew a mechanic to do, who had a very indolent wife; but he seemed not to think it possible. There is such a universal devotion to a particular array of table and table cloths, platters and plates, knives and forks, pots and kettles, and cups and saucers, in New England, that it seems hardly to have entered the minds of people that they can have a comfortable breakfast without them.

But as I have already hinted, my friend Sidney has contrived to get along by his perseverance, and in spite of his wife, who still clings to her bed in the morning; and he is quite a thriving farmer. He has very little affection, it is true, for his wife or his children—having made money his great object.

Were I to be asked what a man should do placed in Samuel Sidney's circumstances, I would say—" Get your own breakfast for a few mornings. You will not suffer—nor will your employer—if you eat from four to eight ounces of good bread, with perhaps a handful of berries or an apple or two; and such a breakfast may be made without the din of pots and kettles." But I seem to forget that I am not writing a book for young husbands.

It is true that breakfast should be, as a general rule, a social occasion, in which much pleasant and agreeable conversation should be elicited; and it will be a work of self-denial for a husband to eat his meal in a solitary manner. But he would not probably be compelled to do so long. This natural punishment of the young wife would probably soon work her reformation. She would not be willing her husband should go without his warm breakfast very long. Or if she had become so thoroughly divested of old prejudices, and so completely reformed in dietetic practice, as to believe that a cold or rather a cool breakfast was better for him and everybody else than a hot one, still she would soon get sick of eating alone, when a little more effort would give to herself and her children the pleasure and the benefit of her husband's company.

I might mention a hundred cases which would show the young wife the importance of early rising, and the dismal consequences which often flow from the neglect of it. But it cannot, surely, be necessary.

CHAPTER XVIII.

INDUSTRY.

An anecdote. Motives to industry. Bible examples of this virtue.

I was acquainted, a few years since, with an old gentleman and lady, both of whom were over ninety years of age. They had lived together seventy years; and yet their whole course had been one of the most untiring industry. They came together, at marriage, nearly as poor as John Bunyan and his wife—that is, almost without knife, fork or spoon—and yet by hard labor and careful management, they have educated—I will not say *well* educated—a large family of children, and acquired considerable property.

They were, I have said, now over ninety years of age. And yet they were still at work; the gentleman on his shoemaker's bench, and the lady at her wheel. "But why do you continue to spin at your age, and in your easy circumstances?" said a neighbor to her one day. "Ah," said she, "it is as much my duty to strain every nerve I have, to lay up property, as it is to go to meeting; and that, not only as a duty to my husband and to society, but to God."

Now this old lady was partly correct, and partly in the wrong. It is indeed true that neither age nor circumstances should prevent our laboring all we can, without injury to our health, and without interference with other duties. But there are a great many kinds of *labor* in this world. Besides this, there are a great many duties devolving upon us not commonly called labor—duties to ourselves, to husbands, and wives, and children, and neighbors, and friends. He who should labor solely to amass property, to the neglect of other duties, would be very far from taking a course acceptable to God.

I rejoice to find persons of ninety years of age, working on and resolved to work on to the end of life; although I am sorry to see them actuated by so low and unworthy a motive as the desire to 'lay up property. I should be glad to have every person, especially every young wife, feel that every " nerve should be strained," as the old lady expressed it, in doing one thing or another.

Spinning is so far out of date, that it might be useless for me to recommend it to the young wife to betake herself to her wheel any part of the day. And yet very few kinds of exercise within doors, are better for many of the class of females for whom

I am writing, than spinning wool, &c., on an old fashioned wheel.

Cookery, when performed on rational principles, is also a valuable employment in point of health; and so are nearly all the various employments which, sixty years ago, devolved on our female community.

But every female is bound to attend to the means of improving her health, as well as of cultivating her own mind and heart. She owes the same duties, moreover, to those around her, especially to her own children. She has duties to perform to the sick and to the well—to the young and to the aged; duties even to domestic animals. Very few of these duties are favorable to the laying up of much property, and some are opposed to it. So that while we commend industry—of the most untiring kind, too—we would neither commend nor recommend strong efforts to lay up property.

Let her, however—to repeat what I have already said—be constantly employed. Let everything be done, too, orderly and methodically. Let her be punctual, eminently so, in the performance of all her engagements. Thus will she strengthen the hands and encourage the heart of her husband, and set an example that she will not be ashamed to have her children follow, and hand down to future and distant generations. Let her be industrious for the sake of the good mental and moral effects which industry produces, and because it is the will of God concerning us, rather than because of its emoluments. These last are not indeed to be despised, even, by the housewife; but it is less safe to overlook them wholly, than to overrate them.

It will be seen by the foregoing remarks, that while industry from proper motives is commended, it is not considered as necessarily a virtue. The adversary of mankind, the devil, is represented in Holy Writ as industrious; none more so, unless it be those friends of man, the seraphs, represented to us flying through the midst of heaven to preach the everlasting gospel. And yet it is presumed no one ever thought of regarding the untiring efforts of a demon, in endeavoring to destroy and devour, as praiseworthy. And yet, must they not be so regarded, if industry is a virtue, independent of the motive which dictates it? It is industry in well doing which is commendable—not industry in doing wrong, or even in the performance of anything at hap-hazard.

To conclude. Our young housewife will do well to study the character of some of the excellent women of old, whose lives are recorded in sacred and profane history. Solomon's description of a virtuous woman includes, as a prominent trait, untiring industry. I wish it were more read and studied. Let females be industrious as she was, for the sake of pleasing God and promoting the happiness of their husbands and families, and let their industry be directed by wisdom, and we need not fear for the results. The following chapter will, it is believed, afford her many useful hints and directions.

CHAPTER XIX.

DOMESTIC ECONOMY.

Economy a word of broad meaning. Much of this chapter anticipated. Servants—their general employment to be regretted. Spirit of the times—illustrated by an anecdote. American nobles. Servants cannot always be dispensed with. Seven reasons for avoiding them, if possible. 1. They are unnecessary. 2. Costly. 3. Break in upon the order of families. 4. Create distinctions in society. 5. Are bad teachers. 6. Practice anti-republican. 7. It is unchristian. Waste of time in cookery. What useful cookery is. Other wasteful practices. Morning calls. General remarks. An anecdote.

THE word economy is one of very extensive meaning, and in its largest sense, would comprise a wide range of female duty. It not only includes the judicious management of pecuniary matters, but the management, regulation and government of a family, or the concerns of a household. It might include, too, a due regard to the health; but of the latter I shall treat in another place. At present, I shall endeavor to confine my remarks to what is usually and more appropriately called domestic economy, or the general management of household concerns.

DOMESTIC ECONOMY. 153

Much of what should otherwise have been presented under this head, has been anticipated in the chapters on Early Rising, Punctuality, Order and Method, and Industry. She who rises late cannot possibly be a good domestic economist, however excellent her management may be in all other respects. A defect so glaring as this cannot be compatible at all with female duty.

Similar remarks might be made in reference to punctuality, industry, order and method. So far as these things are duly regarded by a wife, she is truly economical. But without these virtues and habits, she must fall greatly short of that point, even though she should possess many of the highest excellencies. But as these traits of character have been already considered, the range of my remarks under the head of economy will be somewhat limited.

One of the first things which sound economy demands in a young house-keeper is, to dispense, if possible, with domestics, or servants. I am well aware that there are many difficulties in the way of doing this; nor indeed will it always be practicable, at least in the present state of society. There was a time, in the early history of New England, when the mass of the people—excepting, of course, those who kept boarders, &c.—had no servants from other families. Each family, if in health, performed its own household labor. But those happy days have gone by, and with them, much of the republican spirit and manners which then prevailed. We are beginning, strongly, to imitate foreign manners and customs, not only in city but in country—in the foreground of which is the fashion of having a troop of domestics around us.

I know of many a family, even in some of the country towns of Massachusetts, who constantly employ from one to three hired females, when I am fully confident there is not the least necessity in the world for any. Had such families employed but a single servant, sixty or eighty years ago, they would probably have been laughed at. What then but a servile imitation of and devotion to Fashion, the reigning goddess, has produced a change so universal and so lamentable?

This change has not only affected the wealthier portion of our once frugal, and economical, and happy community, but those in middling and even low circumstances. You will often find the same spirit prevailing among those who are not fairly able to employ a servant regularly, as well as among those who employ fully half a dozen. The same, did I say? I recall the expression. It is a spirit far worse. It is a tone and spirit and manner as much more lordly and haughty than that of those who are really the "nobility" of the community, as can be conceived. The housewife who is resolved to ape the fashions of the great, will be less familiar with her wash-woman, whom she employs in her family once a week, than the mistress of half a dozen regular servants is with them. The latter fears not the loss of rank or dignity, if she converses with her domestics in a familiar manner, and appears to remember that they are made of one blood with herself; but the former, conscious that her hold on nobility is more precarious, is more fearful of losing it by any apparent condescension.

The following is an example of that state of public sentiment which I have been attempting to describe. It is not a creature of the imagination, but is strictly and literally true, except that I have used fictitious names:

Mrs. Williams keeps no servants, but the reason is that she cannot afford it. Her husband and she came together, about two years since, nearly as poor as poor could be; and his present income, in a village of ten or twelve thousand people, is only about $300 a year. This compels them to live not only in a hired house, but in a mean, unhealthy and immoral part of the village—to occupy but a very small space—to dispense with tea and coffee, and to practice many other retrenchments.

I say it *compels* them to do so ; but I do not of course mean that there is any actual compulsion. Mrs. W. is extremely avaricious, and would submit to almost anything to save a dollar or two, with a view to her future aggrandizement ; and to this end, is willing to deny herself almost everything which, in other circumstances, she would heartily desire. She will scarcely suffer her husband to buy a useful book once a year, or subscribe for a newspaper or magazine of any sort ; and she almost grudges the postage on those which are sent them gratuitously.

And yet she will not, if she can find any excuse for avoiding it, perform her own household work. But as she is not able to keep a regular servant, she employs a very worthy but poor woman in the neighborhood, one or two days in the week, to do her principal work—making a shift to get along with the rest of her labor by herself.

But what crowns all, and what is the main object of this narrative, is, that she evidently regards it as beneath her dignity to hold the least conversation—even for a moment—with the lady she employs, except to say yes or no, or to issue her commands. And although the " great work " is performed, to save fuel, in the same room which Mrs. W. and her husband occupy, at meals and at other times, and although the hired lady is as *really*

DOMESTIC ECONOMY. 157

one of the nobility as herself, and much more so, she will no more let her eat at the same table with the family, than if she were of some other race of animals; nor will she permit her husband or others, if she can help it, to speak to her. She would deem it, as I have already said, a loss of dignity.

Now this case, though it may be an extreme one, shows what sort of a spirit is fostered in the community, by the practice of keeping servants—by rendering it, I mean, the universal practice, without any reference to circumstances. It is not merely to impose upon us the proud, aristocratic spirit of the nobles of the old world, but one which is far worse. Where nobility is hereditary, no one fears that a little condescension will injure him. He may talk to a servant or a beggar, and yet be a noble, still. But as what I call nobility, here, is usually acquired, and may therefore be lost, our nobles are more cautious with whom they associate. And it is this cautious spirit, most observable, perhaps, in those who are conscious of their own ill desert, which makes republican nobles so much more proud, and haughty, and intolerable than monarchical ones.

Let me not be misunderstood on this subject. It is far from being my intention to say, or to intimate, that all families, even in the country, can, as society now is, wholly dispense with foreign aid and assistance; much less, that they can do so in the city. Many a young wife has been so trained, that to require her, at once, to perform the household labor, even of her own small family, would be to impair her slender health. That system of training is indeed wrong which produces such results, and it may perhaps be wrong to become the heads of families in such circumstances; but whether it is so or not, is a question which will not be discussed in this place. We are compelled, in some respects at least, to take the world and the things in it as they are. In circumstances like those I have just alluded to, in case of the sickness of one or more members of the family, and in the case of keeping boarders of any kind, or of sustaining public houses of entertainment, I do not see how it is possible to dispense with assistance. The introduction of foreign members into a family, especially of the male sex, demands the introduction of foreign aid, to perform the increased necessary labor.

The following are some of the reasons why I could wish the young wife, who would consult true economy, to dispense, as much as possible, with servants:

1. They seem to me, as a general rule, unnecessary. Are not two healthy persons, of adult

years, able to take care of themselves? What necessity of servants can possibly exist? Have not some of the happiest and most flourishing communities dispensed with them? Is it not true, even now, that the people of the United States enjoy social and domestic happiness just in proportion to their independence of foreign aid, in the management of their households?

2. They are costly. Even a strong British writer seems to admit that "servants are great plagues;" and it is a pretty common maxim with us, that they are about as much trouble as they are worth. But they ought to be of very great real worth, in a pecuniary point of view, to counterbalance the immense evils they produce in other respects—some of which will be mentioned presently. One writer, after a long series of estimates of the actual expense of servants to a family, in dollars and cents, thus remarks:

"Besides the wages, board and lodging of a female servant, there must be a fire solely for her, or else she must sit with the family, and hear every word that passes between them, or between them and their friends. Besides the blaze of coals, however, there is another sort of flame that she will inevitably covet. In plain language, you have a man to keep, a part, at least, of every week; and the leg of lamb, which might have lasted you and your wife three days, will by this gentleman's sighs be borne away in one. Shut the door against this intruder, and out she goes herself; nor will she go empty handed.

"When I lived a short time in S—— Street, following my habit of early rising, I used to see the servant maids, at almost every hour, dispensing charity at the expense of their masters, long before they, good men! opened their eyes. Meat, bread, cheese, butter, coal and candles, all came with equal freedom from these liberal hands. Where there is one servant, it is worse than where there are two or more; for, happily for their employers, they do not always agree; so that the oppression is most heavy on those who are least able to bear it, and particularly on clerks, and such like people."

3. Employing servants breaks in upon the order of families. The general rule, as I have already said, it appears to me should be, for each family, in ordinary circumstances, to take care of itself. By what right, then, can one family claim part of the services of another? And why should A. be entitled to the services of a member of B.'s family, any more than B. is entitled to those of one of the members of the family of A. In other words, if a family is to be broken in upon, who is to decide whose it shall be? Let it be remembered, I

repeat it, that I speak now of things as they generally are. If a family is sick, the order of that family is already broken ; and whether they make the demand or not upon our charity, christianity does. And if we break in upon families by requiring that a large number of boys—no matter whether they are apprentices, students, mechanics or manufacturers—shall board in one building or establishment, then must we break in upon the order of other families, in order to obtain aid in taking care of them.

Divine Providence seems to have made the necessary provision, in all ordinary cases, for every ordinary exigency. If the sons of a family remain, after marriage, in the family of their fathers, or what is the same thing, if the parents live with their children, each young couple will receive considerable aid, during their first years after setting out in life, from their parents. This was, as it appears, the patriarchal plan. The grand-parents, parents and children resided in one family, in one establishment, and thus they could render each other those services which the God of nature intended. I suppose it to be part of the divine intention, that the young should honor the old by cheering and sustaining them ; but can they do it according to that intention, if they are widely separated ?

I repeat it, therefore, that the husband and wife, with the occasional assistance of the old people, can sustain their own families, for a time. And whenever the young family becomes somewhat numerous, and the cares of life begin to press upon parents and grand-parents, the labors of the older children begin to come in, and to be a valuable contribution This is the way, I conceive, in which the great Author of nature makes provision, in a natural state of society, for all those services of others which, in ordinary circumstances, are required.

Let me not be told, in reference to the patriarchs, that even they—Abraham, for example—had numerous servants. These were unnecessary, and were often very costly to them. Who can estimate the mischiefs that grew out of these servants' quarrels, in connection with the history of Abraham, in the separation between him and Lot, and the subsequent miseries of the family of the latter.

4. Employing servants increases the distinctions already sufficiently apparent in society. The more servants there are, the less will there be of self-respect among that class of the community in general, as well as among those with whom they associate. They become more envious and jealous of the rich, and act more and more as spies

upon them. And finding themselves less respected, they become gradually less worthy of respect. So true is this, that it is not uncommon for the mistress of an English household to keep everything locked up, to remove from them all temptation to pilfer. A female writer, of late, not only mentions this circumstance, but apologizes for its supposed necessity. But we need not go to written authorities on the subject. We may know its truth from facts within the range of our own daily observation. Many a house-keeper will at least tell you, (if she does not quite accuse her servants of dishonesty,) that they are so wasteful she cannot trust them with anything more than she is compelled to do, from day to day, or from meal to meal.

This is a most deplorable state of things. But deplorable as it is, it is a very common condition, in fashionable life. And what is still more to be deplored, it is everywhere increasing.

5. Servants are bad teachers and educators. Some may wonder what I mean by speaking of servants as teachers. Yet, is it not well known that *they* are the most effectual teachers of all, who do most towards forming the character? And is it not equally well known that, in many families where servants are employed, the latter, by their influence, do more towards moulding—shaping—

the young human being, than the parents? It is not the instruction of the schools, or of set lessons or precepts at home, that does most towards making us what we are, in real character;—it is the ten thousand little things of life, of whose influence we are usually unsuspecting. Now God has appointed the parents to be the educators of their own children. He has said, Train up or bring up *your* children—not delegating the task to other people—in the nurture and admonition of the Lord. How can a parent be willing to disobey this command, without the most imperious and even extraordinary necessity? Yet, is it not true that every parent does this, who brings up his children where they are under the usual influence of servants?

It was not my object to bring the charge against servants that, besides setting a bad example, they do sometimes inculcate, directly, such habits, and practices, and principles, as should make every virtuous parent shudder. And yet it can be proved. There are on record quite too many cases which go to show that many a son—to say nothing at all of daughters—has been ruined for this world, if not for the next, by the wicked (one might almost say diabolical) conduct of vicious domestics, and even in some few instances, by females.

Nor is it to be forgotten, that servants educate, in a greater or less degree, the older members of our families. It is impossible not to be influenced more or less by them, be our age or circumstances what they may. Our food, our drink, the air we breathe, the clothes we wear, depend more or less for their excellence or want of excellence, on those who prepare them for our use. How much is the human character, at any period of life, though much more in early youth, affected by the quality and condition of the food we eat, the purity or impurity of the water we drink, and the proper ventilation and cleanliness of our rooms! So long as all these, and a thousand other things of daily occurrence, continue to modify our feelings, and ultimately to form or change our character, and so long as these matters are entrusted to the management of servants, just so long will it be true that they educate us.

I know it may be thought, by many, that I carry these matters too far. But I am confident it is not so. Strict justice requires that they should be carried still further. I have heard it ably maintained, and, as I think, *proved*, that no person but a wife or a mother ought to make the bread of her own family. And just as surely as bread is the "staff of life," that is, stands first in our family arrangements as an article of diet, just so surely is the sentiment I have advanced just and defensible.

6. But the system of keeping servants in our families seems to me highly anti-republican. Is it not so? Can it indeed be otherwise? Do not all conscientious parents know that by having a class of persons about them whom they are accustomed to regard as inferiors, they are fostering in their own bosoms, as well as cherishing in the bosoms of their children, if they have any children in the family, a feeling which is as contrary to true republicanism as light is to darkness? It is true that I am not here writing for the young mother; but I wish the young wife to form no habits which the young mother would not be willing to follow. But is the latter willing to bring up a family of children with servants constantly before them, unless the necessity be obvious and imperious? I care not—in this respect—how excellent their character, provided they are regarded as of inferior rank; for if they are thus regarded, the anti-republican lesson is taught—and taught, too, in the most effectual manner.

Impelled, as she supposes, by these considerations, a lady of my acquaintance proposes to dismiss her domestics. Indeed, she says she has already done so. She has only retained a *girl* to help her a little! It happens, however, that this girl is an individual of nearly one hundred and forty pounds weight, strong and muscular, and able to do the work of two common servants. And as if there were still some misgivings, the lady proposes to dismiss *her* too, before long, and suffer a very poor but respectable widow lady and her daughters to occupy the rear of the building, and do her work for her, and thus remove from her children the sad example of a distinction of rank.—Strange she cannot see that this does not mend the matter at all in point of principle! The distinction of rich and poor, of superior and inferior, of dependent and independent, will remain in all its force, notwithstanding the name. It is a distinction of feeling, of which I complain most; and therefore it is that I am desirous of avoiding, to the utmost of our power, all those externals which lead to it.

7. Lastly, I regard the practice of keeping servants as unchristian. I have seldom known the temper or disposition of the mistress of a family, of her daughters, or of the servants themselves, improved by their condition. It may sometimes happen; but the natural tendencies are all the other way. It is a state of temptation, into which a christian should not wish to be led.

But again. Who has seen the servants kept at home from church on Sunday, and from the lecture on week days, to give place for the regular attendance of the master and mistress, without regretting the supposed necessity, everywhere prevalent, of such a practice? Can a custom be right which thus, in effect, robs so many thousands of our race of those privileges to which they are naturally entitled, as well as ourselves? Do not servants need the blessings of that gospel which is specially designed "for the poor," as much, at least, as their masters?

If special efforts were made by masters and mistresses to instruct, at home, those who perform the labor of their families, and to inculcate upon them that religious truth from which their arrangements exclude them elsewhere, the whole case would be altered. But this, we may be assured, will seldom be done, even by the best disciples of the Saviour. Its difficulties will almost always seem to be, for the time, insurmountable; and thus the whole subject will, in general, be neglected.

The grand objection usually brought against the view I take of the whole subject is, that if the wife in every instance performed her own labor, it would prove the means of throwing multitudes of females out of employment. This would be the immediate tendency, no doubt. But this does not prove that a gradual reformation of the practice would be an evil. There was a time, in the progress of the temperance reformation in this country, when it might have been said with truth that, if no one was henceforth to distil grain into whiskey, multitudes would be thrown out of employment. But would this have been a sufficient reason why a christian should continue to be a distiller? If not, then the mere fact that to cease to have servants would throw a few individuals out of immediate employment, would not be a valid argument against such a course. That a few individuals must suffer, for a time, is of course a less evil than to tolerate a practice which produces great and general suffering through the whole community. Lay aside the practice of having servants, and do the work yourself, and you encourage a general state of things in which the persons now employed in the families of others, would have families of their own; whereas, in the present state of things, the number of the unmarried is continually increasing.

I would not have extended my remarks on servants to such a length, had I not deemed it a subject of vital importance to the happiness—the real happiness, I mean—of every young wife in the community. Should she determine to do the work of the family herself, and commence housekeeping on this principle, she will take a great and important step towards securing her happiness for life.

But there are many more things, of at least minor importance, which remain to be treated under the general head, Economy.

She cannot be the best of domestic economists, who spends half her time, while awake, in mere cooking. That cookery has an important place among her duties, there can be no doubt. As little can it be doubted that great skill is required. The preparation of a good loaf of bread, and the art of boiling, in a proper manner, rice, pulse, potatoes, beets, turnips, onions, &c., demand much more skill than is usually supposed. It was the saying of a maker of apparatus for schools, that almost any person could make apparatus which was complicated, but that there were few to be found who could make a simple thing. And there is some truth in the general principle involved in the statement. It requires as much skill to make good bread as to prepare any dish with which I am acquainted; and there are few, so far as my observation of the matter extends, who understand, thoroughly and scientifically, this invaluable art.

Much time is spent by housewives in mashing, chopping, and bruising food. Every kind of food should be so left by cookery as to task, to their fullest reasonable extent, the masticatory organs—the teeth. And yet, is it not correct to say that three fourths of the effort spent in what is called cookery, has a tendency to encourage the teeth in indolence, or at least a waste of time?

Let us take a brief survey. Here is milk, a food comparatively wholesome, at least for children. Yet how much time is spent in making butter, cheese, porridge, custards, ice creams, &c., which, to say the least, are no better food, for children or adults, than milk. Here is wheat. From this, instead of simple coarse bread, we make fine flour bread, cakes of every kind—some sweet, others only shortened—pie-crust, puddings, dumplings, toast, &c. Instead of plain dishes from Indian meal, we torture it in various ways, and mix it with sundry other articles, and add to it butter, molasses, &c. Instead of eating the simple boiled or roasted potato, we mash it, and add butter, pepper, mustard, vinegar, sauces, gravies or horseradish, and make it into bread, pies, and soups, or mix it with turnips or fish. Even the simple rice cannot be eaten, so we think, without butter, molasses, cream, milk, sugar or honey; nor beans and peas without butter, pork, pepper or vinegar. Nay, even the apple must be changed by baking, roasting, grating, and making into pies, dumplings and birds' nests.* Instead of eating

* A species of pudding made by scooping out apples hollow, and filling them with other materials.

simple meat, boiled, roasted or dried, it must be smoked, and covered with vinegar, pepper, mustard, horseradish, sauce or gravy, or made into pies, hash or sausages.

Then in regard to drinks, instead of simple water, we have an array of instruments and vessels, and herbs, foreign and domestic, for manufacturing, at considerable expense, tea, coffee, shells, chocolate, and so on; and we have pitchers, tumblers, and the like, for beer, cider, wine, and other more offensive mixtures. In short—for this is only a mere specimen—there are scarcely any limits to this department of human folly, nor to the waste of time which it involves, without adding one iota to the sum total—to the aggregate—of that pleasure or happiness to which man's nature is originally entitled. On the contrary, it greatly diminishes both.

Useful cookery, though a curious and important art, is not, by any means, complicated. It consists simply in preparing those substances which God has given us for food, such as the farinaceous vegetables and the fruits, in such a way as is best adapted to the most healthy condition of the human stomach and general system.

There is a great deal of female time taken up in useless, hollow morning calls, and in idle, unmeaning ceremonies. A great deal of waste is also involved in dressing in a manner which is as far removed from nature's simplicity, as is our modern system of cookery. The material, as well as the fashion, not only of every kind of dress, but of all sorts of furniture, is such as to involve, first and last, a great waste of precious and invaluable time.

There is no need of all this. It is pitiable—it is wicked. Woman was never made to be thus trifled with. Her influence is too pervading and too powerful to be expended—three fourths of it at least, and probably nine tenths—in a manner which is not merely useless, but rather quite injurious. We say again, therefore, still more distinctly, that the waste of such a vast amount of female energy and time is not only bad economy, but an offence in the sight of Heaven itself.

In the language of another work, whole years, in the aggregate, of every house-keeper's life, might be saved for the benefit of her race. If the best food now known were in general use, and no other—and if cookery, whenever it could not improve it, were wholly dispensed with, more than half of the female labor now expended might be saved, to be devoted to the more glorious purpose of assisting in elevating and improving the hearts and minds of husbands, brothers, sisters and children, and the world around us. We admit, most cheerfully, that as a means of producing vigorous minds and good hearts, a due attention to food, drink, clothing, &c. is indispensable. It is nothing less than the carrying on of one department of the labor assigned to woman by the Creator—the physical education of herself and of those around her. But to see a patient and laborious female spending nearly her whole time in ministering to the *mere* physical wants of man, in the various stages of his existence—infancy, childhood, youth, manhood and age—and doing all this with the utmost cheerfulness, and without appearing to realize that God has given her a higher and nobler office, or at the least, without finding any time to perform its duties, is indeed most lamentable.

It was observed that woman plods on in the narrow, unworthy track assigned her, with the utmost cheerfulness. She does so; and I have never been more forcibly reminded of the power of habit, than when attempts have sometimes been made to emancipate her. I will mention a case which occurred once, within the range of my own observation.

A lady of my acquaintance had a small number of boarders who were all "temperance folks," in the broadest sense of the term. They not only drank nothing but water, but they abstained from all or nearly all condiments, liquid food and mixtures. They lived chiefly on plain bread, boiled rice, potatoes, beans, Indian cakes and puddings, milk and apples. Even these they usually preferred singly, that is, one at a time, and cold. I do not mean ice-cold, but without much artificial heat.

The result was, that though the lady was at first pleased with the idea of having almost nothing to do in the way of cookery, she at length grew quite tired of the plan. She had a very small family of her own, and she was utterly unacquainted with the means of cultivating or improving the minds or the hearts of even those. She had indeed neighbors to call upon, and friends to receive. Still she had a great deal of spare time left her; and what should she do with it?

There was another trouble. She was extremely fond of displaying her skill in cookery—especially in seasoning and mixing various sorts of food. She was fond of making cakes, pies, toasts and soups; of displaying a great variety upon her table; and of sipping at many things, whether she ate much of either or not. But the simplicity of her boarders gave her little opportunity for the display of skill in her favorite department, besides that it left a blank in her time, and gave her hours of leisure that she knew not how to dispose of.

How much I used to pity her, after I learned from one of her boarders her real condition!—for indeed she was deserving of pity. True, she was paid as much as if her labor had been greater; but such were her habits of industry that this did not satisfy, without an opportunity to *perform* the labor, and to exhibit, from day to day, her skill.

Now this lady's case, after all, was not so very singular. I have heard others say—even those who had the care of children—"Suppose three fourths of the time now spent by females, and wasted, as you call it, were really saved, what could they do with it? Would you have them idle? They are happiest in cooking; they like it best; and that, I think, is their province."

And thus they embrace their chains; and say, practically, "Let us still have our wonted slavery. Do not talk of emancipation. We shall have nothing to do, if emancipated. Better by far to remain as we are."

Reader, whoever you are, if you entertain this sentiment, be persuaded to remember, for one moment, at least, that you have an immortal mind and heart, and that your husband has, too. Remember that these minds and hearts need food, as much as the bodies they inhabit; and blush for shame that your sentiments contemn them as beneath your care. Why, you ought to rejoice with all your hearts, and thank the great Former of both your body and spirit, for every hour of leisure which, in his Providence, he gives you ; and earnestly devote it all to the work of self-improvement and the improvement of your husband. Could you get through with providing for the physical wants of your little family in a single hour, and should your family never be any larger than it now is, you would not have a moment too much of time for a work as much nobler than that which has hitherto engrossed almost your whole attention, as the spiritual part is nobler than the physical tenement which it inhabits.

CHAPTER XX.

DOMESTIC REFORM.

Present state of things. Females ignorant of domestic concerns. A great mistake in education. Nature of the mistake. Cause of the pecuniary distress of our country. Example of ministers. Change or reform necessary. How it is to be effected. By whom begun. The young wife to begin it. She should begin immediately. One serious difficulty. How to overcome it. Gradual reformation. Rapid progress, ultimately. Book learning. How far books are useful. "The Frugal Housewife." "Bread and Bread-making."

In the last chapter, I have, for the sake of brevity, taken it for granted that the young wife understands thoroughly the common duties of domestic life; and have, therefore, dwelt chiefly on the importance of her performing them in her own person, instead of delegating them—as many in these days are inclined to do—to other persons.

But it most unhappily occurs that many a newly married lady is nearly as ignorant of domestic duties, as a child. Perhaps she is not more to blame for it than her parents. Still the evil exists, and that very frequently; and a lamentable evil it is, too. And let the blame be where it may, it demands attention and correction.

Let it not be supposed, from these or any other remarks of mine, that I place too high an estimate on the domestic qualifications and duties of a female. Her intellectual, and social, and moral qualifications are, no doubt, of infinitely more consequence, in themselves considered ; but these depend so much on the proper management of our domestic concerns, that the latter, for the sake of the former, demand much more attention than they appear to me to have hitherto received. Writers on female duty have dwelt at large on almost every topic but this.

I am truly surprised at the mistakes made, in these days, in the education of daughters. Nearly the whole of our females, in the higher walks of life—and not a few others—are educated in an almost entire ignorance of household work and household economy. They are taught everything in the world, rather than that in which, if in nothing else, they ought to excel, were it only for its own sake—but much more for its social advantages.

This, I say, is the result of mistake, and not of intention. You will hardly find a father or a mother who will not regard it, in the abstract, as a capital error. And yet many a parent who abhors it in theory, embraces it in practice.

How can she who has never seen her mother diligently employed in the management of household concerns, be expected to understand them? Can it be expected that she will associate with the servants, voluntarily, to make herself acquainted with such matters? Or if she has even seen her mother engaged in domestic concerns, while she knew she regarded them as mere drudgery, and was miserable all the time she was employed in them, will she be likely ever to understand them?

How can she who is always at school—save what time she spends in eating, dressing, visiting and sleeping—ever understand and love the employments of the kitchen? Is the love of domestic life so congenial to our nature as to grow up uncultivated, and even in spite of cultivation?

I have no objection to books and schools;—far from it. But the introductory school room, to the young female, is the kitchen; and some of the first lessons are in making bread, making, mending and washing clothes, cleansing furniture, &c.

One cause of those seasons of pecuniary and commercial embarrassment, which have become, of late, so frequent and so distressing in our country, is to be found in the error in female education to which I allude. There are whole classes, or nearly whole classes of our community, with whom domestic concerns—instead of being regarded as a means of promoting health and happiness—are considered as a grievance. Perhaps I ought not to select any one class, where the classes to which I refer are so numerous—but if I were to do so, I would first select ministers. I would do so, not only because the error is with them quite prominent, but because it is propagated at a most rapid rate, by their example.

How rare is it for a minister to marry a lady who understands, and above all, who loves the domestic concerns of a household? There was a time in the history of our country, when daughters of rank were trained like the rest of their fellow beings. At least, this was the case with a proportion of them, in country places. I have known many a minister's wife, whose hands performed all the labor of her family, while in health. Nor was this labor incompatible with a good degree of mental improvement. It gave her a vigorous body, and at the same time, vigor of mind; and when she read, or meditated, or conversed, she was truly intelligible, as well as in earnest.

But it is not so now. Ministers' wives and daughters would be degraded—so says fashion—by domestic care. And as the clergy are—in a country where they have, and should have, very great influence—so, in no small degree, are the people. At least, what it is deemed disgraceful to their wives or daughters to do, is soon deemed disgraceful to the wives and daughters of others. And one consequence is, that what are thought the necessary expenses of families have increased, to an extent that is truly alarming. We are told about the evils of speculation—and they are indeed terrible; but they are only as spots in the social horizon. The evils of extravagance in our houses, our equipage, our household arrangements, our furniture, our dress, &c, are as a thick cloud which casts a shade over the whole face of things, and darkens all our present and future prospects.

Our country never will be happy, till the present tendency of things is changed; till ministers and other professions and classes of men, set the example of honoring domestic labor; till every wife and daughter is taught to perform—and with pleasure and alacrity, too—the domestic concerns of a household. I do not say that if this change were effected—if every mistress of a family rose early, and, like the virtuous woman described by Solomon, applied herself diligently to labor, and taught her daughters to do and love the same—our country would at once return to its primitive happy condition. There are numerous other causes of present trouble to be removed. But I do say that this is one *primary* cause of the present suffering; and that we cannot have permanently happy times, till this cause, among others, is removed.

Now, how is the change to be effected? Not, surely, by any one individual. No person has so much influence—at least I suppose so—that her example, alone, would accomplish the whole work. There must be multitudes engaged in it. There must be a general attack on a habit which is productive of so much social and moral mischief.

But how shall the work begin? Though no one can perform the whole of it, by herself; somebody must begin it. On whom devolves the duty and the task? Who shall apply to the great mass of society that leaven which may gradually extend its influence till the whole is leavened?

It is true that the more influence a person has in society, the greater is her power to effect, by her example, a reform. Yet it often happens that the individual who might have most influence for good in society, cannot be enlisted in the cause. She is already employed on the other side, and can hardly be drawn off. Shall we wait for her? What is our hope? What reason is there for believing she will ever change? Certainly none which is derived from the past.

The conclusion is, then, that *she* must commence the work, who is convinced of its importance. She must commence it, who feels that it ought to be commenced. It is of little comparative consequence how slender or how unimportant her influence. She can never know that her single example may not be the very point from which, as from a radiating centre, the work of social reformation is to proceed. It is not necessary that she should know. Let her do her duty. Let her begin. Her example—the sacrifice—if she do not effect the whole object, cannot be lost. And it may, as I have already said, be the very hinge on which the whole reformation of society is to turn. A word, it has been said, may move a continent; —how much more an action; or what is more, a series of actions!

She may find her success far greater than she anticipates. Though she may not be the wife of a minister, some minister's wife may take courage from her example. People are not so ignorant of the true method of reform, as they are wanting in moral courage to begin it. There are multitudes who are almost ready to begin, by their example, if they dare to be singular. Some would begin, if they had but one person to accompany them. Others, in still greater numbers, would begin if there were two to join them. Others still, if the number of reformers were still greater. But the trouble is to find a person who dares to place herself foremost in the conflict. Let this individual be found, and I hesitate not to say that the work of reform is, prospectively, accomplished.

Let the individual, then, I again say, who has read the chapter which precedes this, and who feels that society is getting radically wrong on the subject of domestic arrangements and domestic management, resolve to begin, in her own family, the work of reformation. Let her resolve to begin it now. Let her resolve, too, on something more than a mere beginning. She must determine to carry it through. Her influence may not be felt in a month, or a year. People may regard it, for a time, as a freak. But when they see her going steadily on, from year to year, in her new course, their confidence will be increased, and they will venture to join her.

If these remarks should be the means of enlisting the moral courage of but one young wife, and and of leading her to undertake, in her own little sphere, the work of reform, how great beyond expression will be my reward. And if that individual should be the means, under God, of effecting so great and needful a change in society, how great will be the reward of her labors and sacrifices, both in time and in eternity. Nay, should she be compelled to stand alone through life—a thing which can hardly happen—she will have greatly blessed herself and her family, and her example will have its influence on those who come after her.

There is, however, one important preliminary to her attempting this work of reformation. She must secure not only the approbation, but the cooperation of her husband. How difficult a task this may be, will depend upon circumstances. There are husbands who prefer that their wives should be mere dolls as long as they live, let the hazard or evils be what they may. There are others who would like the reformation, but will not be willing you should be over-active in it. In either of these cases, your condition will be almost hopeless. It is enough for you to have the rest of the world against you. To have your husband against you with the rest, would be a condition most unhappy indeed. If you can, by degrees, bring over such a husband to your own opinion, very well; but if not, it is perhaps better that nothing should be attempted.

But the majority of husbands, it is to be hoped, will need no arguments to induce them to cooperate. They are, for the most part, if their professions are sincere, ready and anxious to sustain you in all your efforts; and to do, with their own

DOMESTIC REFORM.

hands, not a little to encourage you, and to lessen the daily amount of your labors.

Suppose, however, you are not only ready to begin the work of reformation, but to begin it immediately. *How* is it to be done? You have a servant, it may be, in your family. Shall you turn her away at once, and do the work yourself? Or will it be best to begin gradually? If you have never been accustomed to labor, a gradual commencement will be best and safest. Let your help remain, for a time, to teach you what you do not know, and to perform what you cannot do. If they dislike this—a thing not at all unnatural to persons in these circumstances—and gradually become very uneasy and unhappy, it will, of course, be better to dismiss them, and do the best you can. Your husband and yourself may manage, for a time, with very little household labor—putting out, as you probably would, your heavier work;—and your strength and skill would be every day increasing.

If you are anxious to make progress, and especially at your age, your improvement, under the circumstances I have mentioned, will be exceedingly rapid. It is a pretty common saying, that people may become what they desire to be. This saying, if it be not true to the utmost, has a great deal of truth in it. If you have set your heart on becoming a thorough, experimental housewife—if you have taken it up as a matter of christian duty to yourself and family, and if, above all, you have taken it up in the hope of influencing others by your example, your motives will be so numerous and so powerful, as to impel you onward with a rapidity of which, before this, you had no conception.

One reason why young girls, especially the girls of modern times, are so exceedingly slow in acquiring the art of housewifery is, that they have no powerful commanding motives to urge them along in the path of progress. Sweeping and washing and cooking are irksome, because they esteem it a drudgery; and they esteem it a drudgery, because those around them esteem it so, too. What wonder that, under these circumstances, they learn slowly, and, indeed, seldom, if ever, become skilful! Besides this, most girls think that they can quickly learn to do house-work, at any time, should their circumstances make it necessary for them to do so.

I have said that your progress will be rapid, if you are determined on improvement, and are willing to improve by personal experiment. You may, however, learn a great deal from the experience of others. And this, I take it for granted, you will be willing, and even glad to do. I take it for granted you are not one of those who, if they cannot find out a thing of themselves, choose to remain in ignorance.

There are not a few to be found, who are exceedingly prejudiced against learning from the experience of others, when it happens to be in a book. They are quite willing to learn from observation, and even from conversation. Nay, they will receive, with great pleasure and confidence, stories of the experiments of ignorant and not very credible persons, when they have them by word of mouth; but the moment they see an account of an experiment in a book, let the author be ever so credible, they start back from it in disgust, and say it is book-learning, and therefore good for nothing. The cry against book-learning, in farming and house-keeping, has had quite a run in this country. I hope, however, for the honor of human nature, it is now nearly over.

Book-learning alone—that is, the written experience of others, without the aid of our own experience and observation—is a very poor affair indeed. I should as little value a housewife or a farmer, whose knowledge consisted merely in the study of books, and who had no common sense, as I should a physician or a lawyer of the same description. Art improves nature; but art without nature is worse than useless. In like manner, the experience of others, whether written down in books or not, is of very great value, to polish and improve and assist our own experience.

I have made these remarks as an introduction to what I am going to say to the young wife whose education has been so defective, as to leave her ignorant on the subject of house-keeping. I would have her study the subject—and that, too, most thoroughly. Such works as the "Frugal Housewife" are valuable, and will afford her great aid. But something more philosophical will still be necessary. She needs a profound knowledge of domestic chemistry, as well as of the intimate structure and laws of life, or animal and vegetable anatomy and physiology.

Although the whole of our life does not consist in mere eating, yet our food, in its quantity and quality, has much—very much—to do with our health and happiness; and the good housewife should pay special attention to this department, as one of great importance to a family. The books in this country—at least, all I have seen—which treat on this subject, embody so much of human experience in the preparation of foolish or hurtful mixtures, that I am sometimes disgusted with the whole of them, and led to believe that they do more harm than good. And yet treatises on the important art of cooking, in the most healthy manner, plain and appropriate articles of food—treatises, I mean, which are founded in true science, or are the result of extensive practice, can never be too numerous. Among this class is a small work on "Bread and Bread Making," lately published in this city, with which every house-keeper who undertakes the work of reform, either with a view to her own happiness or that of others, ought to be familiarly acquainted.

CHAPTER XXI.

SOBRIETY.

Definition of the term. Something more than temperance. Tea drinking. Effects of tea and coffee. Physiology of their effects. Nervous excitement—compared with intoxication. Proofs of the author's views. Sobriety at feasts. Sobriety in company. Other forms of sobriety.

LET not the reader startle, as if he supposed I was going to charge the female sex with the grosser forms of intemperance—with downright drunkenness. Far enough from that. Not but that there are individuals among the sex who have sunk thus low—a few, even of those who are dignified with the sacred and responsible name of wife. But such cases, in our New England community, are so rare, and in general, so inaccessible, that I will not spend strength or time, at least at present, in dwelling upon them. Not one in ten would ever read my remarks, and not one in a hundred who did would be benefited by them.

But there are some forms of intemperance, properly so called, to which females—some too who are in general truly respectable—do not hesitate to descend. There are even a considerable number who use, or who countenance the use, as a beverage—which is nearly the same thing—of several sorts of fermented liquors. There are those who drink wine, cider and beer, and give it to their friends; and there are also those who laugh at what they call the squeamishness or the ultraism—but which may, for aught they can know, be the conscientiousness—of those who do not. But I am willing to pass over this also, for there is another form of intemperance still more common, and in which most young wives with whom I am acquainted participate.

I allude here to the use of coffee and tea, those common beverages of New England. I maintain, whatever may be thought to the contrary, that the use of these articles, for any other than medicinal purposes, is neither more nor less than a species of intemperance.

They excite the brain and nervous system, just as other intoxicating liquors do. And what difference does it make whether the excitement be produced by one drink or another? If rum, gin, brandy, whiskey, cider, beer, coffee and tea are each and every one of them drunk for the sake of the excitement they produce on the nervous system, why is not one as much an intoxicating liquor as the other?

I do not mean to say that a single cup of tea or coffee, or a single half pint of cider or beer, will produce as great a *degree* of intoxication as the same quantity of rum or brandy—for every one knows better. But I do mean to affirm that people use these drinks chiefly, if not wholly, on account of the exciting or intoxicating properties they contain; and that no female who uses any of them freely can be, in the fullest sense of the term, a person of sobriety.

Does any person believe otherwise? Does any one suppose she drinks these beverages to quench thirst? Does any individual believe she would drink them long, if their intoxicating or exciting properties were omitted, though the rest of the properties of the beverage were to remain?

Much is said about their giving strength; and yet they make not—they never did make—a particle of blood. There is no nutriment in tea or coffee—at least, so far as we consider them as mere drinks. But suppose there were;—we need not use them for the sake of that nutriment, since we could get the same or a much greater amount of nutritious matter, by eating a small quantity of solid food.

But I say again, we do not drink coffee or tea for the sake of the nutriment they afford. We drink them to excite us. This excitement may, it is true, be mistaken by some for permanent strength. But it is not so. It is mere nervous excitement, and nothing more. It operates as all unnatural excitement does. It operates, in a greater or less degree, very much as fermented or spirituous liquors, or opium, or tobacco do. It seems to give strength; and perhaps, by exciting the nerves or brain, or both, does so for a short time; but as it does not and cannot make a particle of new blood, nor improve the condition of any particle already made, the strength it gives is quite evanescent. Indeed, it weakens us in the end;— not so much by taking away our muscular strength, as by weakening our cerebral and nervous systems, and diminishing the sum total of our nervous energy.

When, therefore, I hear people say that they must have their tea or their coffee, or they could not work, they should faint, &c., or when I hear them say that tea, at the close of a hard day's work, rests and refreshes them, or takes away the nervous headache, or removes their drowsiness,— instead of hailing it as a messenger of good to mankind, I always shudder at the thought of the mischief it involves. And coffee is as bad as tea. Dr. S., a very distinguished physician of Boston, says it is worse, and that its use is one of the most serious evils in the community.

It is true, people are sometimes faint with labor, and tea or coffee will restore, suddenly, their strength; but so would a certain dose—in some more, in others less—of spirit, or opium, or camphor. It is true that it rests them, when they are tired, and keeps them wakeful when they feel inclined to sleep; but it is also true that it ought not to do so. What they want is sleep and rest—not food or drink, nor any other refreshment. It is true, moreover, that tea or coffee may take away, for the time, the nervous headache, and promote digestion; but it is equally true, that they leave the system, as soon as their first effects are gone, in a much worse state than they found it. In short, it is thus true that these drinks produce many of the effects attributed to them; but they do it by inducing a species of intoxication.

I repeat it, every one of these exciting drinks—and all kinds of food, especially all condiments—that removes faintness, gives a sudden appetite, restores immediate strength, removes headache, &c., does it by a slight degree of intoxication. And can females use intoxicating drink, as a common beverage, and yet be properly considered as persons of sobriety?

If any individual doubts the correctness of these views, let him watch the effects of small quantities of each of the drinks I have included under the name of intoxicating liquors. Let him watch the beer drinker, the wine or cider drinker, the moderate spirit drinker, and the tea or coffee drinker. Will he not perceive the effect, in all, to be in some respects the same?

What is the difference, in nature, between the effects of two liquors, one of which is drank before a meal, and the other with it, while both loosen the tongue, fire the eye, produce mirth and wit, excite the animal passions, and lead to remarks about ourselves and others, that we should not have made in other circumstances, and which it were far better for us and the world, never to have made? Is one sex to be regarded as intemperate, in the use of an article which makes them talkative, while the other sex, excited in the same manner, and rendered talkative in the same manner, by the use of another article, is to be considered sober?

I am for encouraging social visits—ay, and social feasts, too—if conducted on christian principles. Perhaps it is even desirable that woman, shut out of active life as she is, should expend a larger share of voluntary power than man, through the muscles concerned in speech; but is it desirable that she should intoxicate herself in order to excite her talkative or risible faculties? And if she does so, must not every considerate person regard it as a manifest breach, not only of decorum, but of sobriety?

But this giddy, noisy mirth, as I have already intimated, may be excited by eating to excess, or by eating things improper to be eaten. The gluttonous are as truly guilty of a breach of sobriety as those who abuse themselves by improper drinks.

I have seen young married ladies who seemed to regard their new condition as a species of imprisonment, and the duties of a household as mere penance. They would attend to them, perhaps, if they could not help it; but as to finding anything like enjoyment in them, they did not. They were only happy when they were skipping, romping and capering, or at least gadding. Their levity even extended so far, in some cases, as to excite feelings in their companions against which it was their highest duty, no less than their deepest interest, to guard. Here, too, was a want of what I call sobriety. There was the absence of that "steadiness, seriousness, carefulness, and propriety of conduct" which, in a young wife, are exceedingly becoming, and without which, I can never regard her as a truly sober woman.

Sobriety, in short, is a word of extensive import. There are those who go not beyond the strictest bounds of propriety in the use of meats and drinks and company, who are yet very far from being habitually sober and discreet. Nor is sobriety synonymous with gravity;—still less, with anything which approximates to melancholy. There is a happy medium between levity and melancholy, that, even in youth and middle age, falls somewhat short of that gravity, to which the young wife should aspire. It always pleases, cheers, improves, adorns, exalts. It is favorable to health, peace, social comfort, happiness and piety.

CHAPTER XXII.

DISCRETION.

Paul's estimate of the importance of discretion. Opinions of Gisborne. Various forms of indiscretion. Danger of extremes. What true purity is. A word of caution to the indiscreet.

If the apostle Paul, in his letter to Titus, after having directed that young women should be instructed to be sober, does not regard it as trifling to speak of the importance of discretion, it cannot certainly be amiss for me to add a few words on this quality, and on its value as a means of promoting and upholding matrimonial happiness.

Discretion, says Gisborne, is not one of those virtues which come into practice only in singular conjunctures, under circumstances which can seldom happen to the same individual, and to some persons, may never occur at all. It is not a robe of state, to be drawn forth from its recess on some day of festivity, nor a ponderous cloak, to be put on to repel the violence of a thunder shower. It is to the mind what the every-day clothing is to the body. It is requisite, under every vicissitude, to health, and propriety, and comfort.

Discretion, he continues, embraces every season and every incident of life. At home and abroad, in the city and in the country, with intimates and with strangers, in business and in leisure, it is vigilant, and active, and unwearied. It enhances the utility of virtue, and anticipates the allurements of vice. It attends to persons and feelings, to times, occasions and situations, and abstains from all appearance of evil.

This virtue is the more worthy of being inculcated with earnestness on married people, because they appear, in several respects, to be in greater danger than the single, of being led by custom or hurried by inadvertence to disregard it. The giddy and the vain often indulge themselves, without reserve, in a freedom of manners, and a levity of conversation, from which this fear of incurring censure and exciting disgust had previously taught them to refrain. Plunging with augmented eagerness into the hurry of dissipation, and little scrupulous as to the society with which they tread the circle of amusements, they take fire at each remonstrance of a husband, as a reflection on their character, and feel the smallest obstacle to the career of their pleasures as an act of tyrannical control. Hence while the wife, on the one hand, relies on the innocence of her intentions—and the husband, on the other, has not to charge himself with unkindness or austerity, the secret springs of disquietude and grief, perhaps of indifference, of alienation of heart, and of incurable dissensions, are already opened.

Is the wife then innocent? Unquestionably not. Admit her giddiness and vanity to be no subjects of serious reprehension—no considerable deviations from christian sober mindedness; admit her manners and her conversation to have been clear from every imputation, except that of thoughtless imprudence:—a heavy charge will yet remain. She has wounded the feelings of her husband; she has exposed to risk the warmth of his affection; she has laid herself open to the insinuations of calumny; she has exhibited a dangerous example; she has trodden a most dangerous path; she has hazarded her own happiness, and that of the person most dear to her, by a neglect of discretion.

But the giddy and the vain are not the only married women who are found to be indiscreet in their manners and deportment. Some, whose feelings are not very refined, take scarcely any pains to preserve their discourse and behaviour as pure, and chaste, and correct, as it should be. They do not hesitate to dwell, in common conversation, on acts of misconduct and guilt, from the contemplation of which a mind of innate modesty would at once recoil. They behave to their acquaintance of the other sex, with blunt and unrestrained familiarity. And some are even so blinded as to make their married state an excuse for laying aside that delicacy which they regard as an unnecessary formality.

No doubt, the artificial reserve of former times ought to be discarded. At all events, modesty is not stiffness. There is, however, no little danger of going to the contrary extreme. Odious as formality is, it is better—far better—to be deemed somewhat formal, than to be actually indiscreet. To imagine that a state of life in which your conduct so intimately affects the happiness of another person should lessen your obligations to be discreet and prudent, is a most serious error. What can be more likely to wound the feelings or deaden the affection of a husband, than to perceive his wife daily paying less and less regard to those very qualities which so much endeared her to him before marriage?

It must not be. Marriage does not diminish female obligation in this respect; but, on the contrary, greatly increases it. And there is one fact to be observed in these circumstances, which greatly enhances the value of caution. When we have once gone in the road of indiscretion, it is exceedingly difficult to retrace our steps. Many suppose that though there is no place of repentance to be found for indiscretion before marriage, yet the case is altered afterward. Now the greater evil of indiscreet or unchaste conversation consists in the transgressor's own mind and conscience. These it is which are defiled. And this defilement is not confined to any state of life, married or single; nor is the mind, when once defiled in either case, easily purified again. The stain is apt to abide—sometimes forever.

I tremble for those who do not tremble for themselves, in this matter. The error to which I refer is much more common among us than many persons are aware. If these remarks, and similar ones in the chapter on Purity of Character, should awaken here and there a reader to the importance of a course which will prevent the necessity of repentance, it is all I dare to hope.

CHAPTER XXIII.

SCOLDING.

Many kinds of scolds. Internal scolding. Intermittent scolds. Periodical scolding. Other forms of scolding. Hints over the husband's shoulder.

THERE are many kinds of scolds, as well as varieties of scolding. Some forms of the "disease" are indeed worse than others, and some "patients" who labor under it less tolerable than others. But all forms of the disease are really intolerable, and render those who are "afflicted" intolerable too, for the disease's sake.

Some scold outright. Their fits of peevishness are like the desolating storm or tornado, that sweeps over us, and is then gone—leaving a calm behind, which we even seem to enjoy with greater zest from the contrast. The wise mariner, however, will prefer the steady good weather to the alternation of storm and calm.

Some scold internally. Perhaps they never utter a word which could be called downright scolding; and yet their eyes and countenances and actions tell the story. There are two sorts of these internal scolds. One sort always exhibit the outward signs of an internal and spiritual misery—the depressed and wrinkled brow, the depressed angle of the mouth, and the peculiar turn of the sides of the nose, which indicate, that if the features have not actually grown into a scolding state, they are in great danger of it.

But there is another sort in whom the disorder has seasons of remission. Their countenances, though seriously injured, are not yet permanently contracted. There is yet space for repentance and amendment of life. These might be denominated intermittent scolds.

There are also periodical scolds. Some of these always scold in the morning; and as the sun advances towards the meridian, gradually become cheerful. Others begin their song towards evening, and are most effectually cured by darkness and sleep. Some scold at particular seasons, especially in the spring. Others still, it is said—but I will not vouch for the truth of this—scold most at particular periods of the moon.

There are also many sorts of scolds which cannot be so easily classed. Some habitually scold when they want a new dress. Others scold still worse after they get it, because it is faulty. Some scold because their scolding produces no effect, as it is said the wife of Socrates sometimes did.

Some, in the last place, scold because they do not know any better. They were trained to scold at times at the servants, and would no more think of getting along wholly without scolding than without eating.

I counsel the husband who has married a scold—or would do so, if this were the place to counsel husbands—not to resort at once to the laws of divorce for relief from his unhappy situation; but, if he finds his wife's case remediless, to bear it as well as he can, as a just punishment on him for want of more foresight. And if his wife should fret herself to death early—for all fretting and scolding shortens life more or less—and a second should be resolved on, I counsel him to take a little pains to prevent that which he would afterwards give "a thousand worlds," if he had them, to cure.

CHAPTER XXIV.

FORBEARANCE.

Perfection not to be expected. Maxim of a philosopher. Spirit of forbearance a pearl of great price. Cases where forbearance is required. Triumphing. "I told you so." Comparisons. Joking. Saying of Salzman.

No quality is more frequently demanded in the newly married, than mutual forbearance; and yet none, perhaps, are more liable to be disregarded, especially where little things are concerned. Many a wife as well as husband will exercise the spirit of forbearance in larger matters, and yet make most egregious failures, when smaller matters only are concerned. I shall therefore dwell principally on the latter.

Settle it, therefore, as a principle, that perfection is not a plant of terrestrial growth; and that it will therefore be in vain to expect it in a husband. Of the necessity of mutual concession, I have already spoken. But there is an allowance to be made daily, and sometimes hourly, for each other's failings, which falls far short of what we usually call concession.

I believe it was Epictetus who said that to bear and forbear was the perfection of humanity. Be this as it may, it is a pearl of great price; and to none is it more so than to the young wife. If her expectations of her husband's character and habits have been but moderately raised, she probably will not escape trials; if they have been high, she cannot. It will be the highest wisdom, then, to be prepared to meet them—and to meet them in a becoming manner.

You find your husband addicted to certain low, vulgar or awkward habits of conduct; and you find it next to impossible to break the force of them. You find him addicted, it may be, to bad language—or, at least, language which you would not prefer; and you are laboring to reform him. Sometimes you fear you make no progress, and are nearly discouraged—perhaps almost vexed. But in these circumstances, you should remember, consists your trial. Here it is, precisely, that you are called upon to exercise and to cultivate the spirit of forbearance.

Sometimes your trial is still more severe. There are wives to whom their husbands seem to say— not in words, perhaps, but by their daily practice— Now that we have you in our possession, we are resolved to make you submit to our own course. Nothing, perhaps, will more severely test your forbearance than this assumption, on the part of your husband, that might gives right.

But what will you do? Will you resent it? Suppose your husband uses words which imply a determination to exercise the superiority which he claims; will you "answer a fool according to his folly," or will you bear and forbear?

Some husbands, to show their superiority, are always pretending to greater foresight than you, especially after an event has happened. It seems wonderfully easy for some people to *foresee* events after they have actually happened. "Ah, I thought so," or, "Ah, I told you so," many a husband has said to his wife, when, in fact, he knew no more about the event, before it happened, than the man in the moon.

Even when, by our superior wisdom or better opportunities, we have actually foreseen an occurrence or an evil, which our companion had not foreseen, it is not very agreeable to her to be told so, in the way of triumph. Hardly any little thing will so soon alienate the affections of a friend, as seeming to triumph over him. Zimmerman says it is dangerous to get the better in an argument. And if you would have your husband avoid the frequent use of the little phrase, "I told you so," you must be careful, above all, not to set him a frequent example of its use.

Avoid too many comparisons. Some young wives are ever comparing their condition with what it formerly was, with a view to show how much they have done and sacrificed for their husbands. They might have been the companion of one who lives in a splendid castle, or has risen to a post of honor or usefulness; or they might have had a thousand enjoyments, by remaining at home, of which they are now bereft; or they might have avoided these or those cares, anxieties or trials! You should remember, here, the golden rule; and if comparisons of the kind would be painful to yourself, be careful not to give others pain in the same way. Every situation has its pleasures and advantages; and since you cannot alter what is past, or at least, what is in its nature *un*alterable, this alone is reason enough why you should set a guard over your tongue in this respect, if not over your thoughts.

I do not like to hear a wife say, "You knew all this before you married me." It may be true; but husbands do not like to hear it often. It is better to forbear. Think twice before you speak once, even to him who values your society above all else. "Behold how great a matter a little fire kindleth.—And the tongue is a fire—a world of iniquity."

Slight jokes or repartees may, perhaps, be safely indulged in; but I have heard jokes whose effects were anything but happy. I have known deep and lasting wounds inflicted in this way. Be cautious here, too. Remember you are, in many respects, the teacher of your husband; and remember the saying of an aged German instructor, Salzman, that if a teacher has trouble in his school, he should first look for the cause in himself or his own behaviour, where he will very often find it.

CHAPTER XXV.

CONTENTMENT.

Value of contentment. Why it is especially valuable to the young wife. Duty to her own family and others. Duty to God.

THERE is no situation of human life, however unfavorable, which will not be rendered more tolerable by contentment. This, indeed, is so trite a remark, that it was hardly necessary to repeat it. My only reason for doing so is, that of all or nearly all other persons in the world, contentment is most valuable to the class of persons for whom I am writing.

I have, in a former chapter, alluded to the fact that a young wife, in most cases, gives up, in leaving her native home, many physical comforts, as well as valuable social enjoyments. Besides a mother, a father, brothers and sisters, she has her little circle of acquaintances and distant relatives, some of whom she was accustomed to see two or three times a year, some every month, some every week, others almost or quite every day. Here is an aged grandmother, in whose arms, nearly as much as in those of her mother, she has been brought up, and whom she loves almost as tenderly. There is a dear aunt, and two or three cousins, whose society, occasionally, at least, seems as dear to her as her own existence. There, also, within a mile or two of her native home, settled around, are half a dozen or a dozen of her old play-mates or school-mates, whose faces, and whose society, too, are not so easily relinquished or forgotten.

Nor is this all. She is not only attached to persons, but to things. The parlor, the book-case, the garden, the flowers, yonder ancient cherry tree, the peach trees, the plum trees, the currant bushes, and even the aged elms in front of the house, with the beautiful lawn around, are, from association, almost as dear to her as the persons around whose happy domicile they are clustered. Then there are the school-house, and the church, and the grave-yard, and the green, and the post office. And then, how many pleasant associations cluster around the latter.

There is, I am aware, a very great difference in young ladies, in regard to the strength of these attachments; and there is also a difference, still greater, in regard to the power of forming new ones. But it is seldom given to a young woman to be able to break from the scenes of her youth, and of so much physical comfort, and it may be, of so many means of social, intellectual and moral improvement, without a struggle, and without many sighs and tears. It is indeed right that it should be thus ordered.

But when her decision is made, and the struggle is over, she should study contentment in her new situation. She is not indeed to forget her former home and its joys, but she is to lay the foundation of another, equally happy. *That* home was not formed by herself. It was the workmanship of others, *for* her. And has she nothing to do in return?

Suppose she and all other daughters were to cling for life to the old domicile, disregarding the virtual injunctions of the great Creator, and passively occupying seats or reclining in bowers prepared for them. Suppose they were to have no reference to the future—to those who should come after them? What, at this rate, would become of the world? And is it not manifestly—I repeat the sentiment—the duty of the young wife, to do her part in preparing for others, what has been, at so much expense, prepared for herself?

Besides, it is not only Bible doctrine, but the plainest injunction of common sense—elevated and rational common sense, I mean—that "it is more blessed to give than to receive"—that though we may receive and enjoy much good in a passive state at home, yet such is the arrangement of Divine Providence, that we shall enjoy much more of happiness in action—in doing—than in mere receiving.

Perhaps some young wives will remember this. Perhaps they will try to recollect that though there is enjoyment in receiving, there is still more in giving;—yes, and more love, too—genuine, rational love of others. But I have explained and illustrated this doctrine in another chapter. All the use I wish to make of it here is, to apply it to the case of forming a new family, and creating, as it were, a circle or scene of new joys and attachments. Great as the pleasure is which we receive in a domestic circle prepared for us, that is unquestionably greater, which we derive from preparing one of our own. More than this, it is the very doing something for others, at least in part, which makes us love them. We love our friends, it is true, anterior to doing anything for them; but we love them much—I was going to say infinitely—better, when we have done our duty to them as parents, or husbands, or wives, through a long series of years.

It should also help to render the young wife contented, that, in leaving her native home, she is conforming to the will of God. For it cannot, it seems to me, be doubted what the will of God is, in this matter. Woman, like man, has a mission; and to exercise or fulfil it requires that, like Abraham and others, she should leave friends and kindred, and go out into the wide world, she sometimes knows not whither. But if she has been wise and careful and prayerful in her determination; if she has consulted duty, as a principal thing, rather than inclination, or at least, rather than fancy; and if she has that trust in Heaven which she needs in all situations, but especially in matrimony, she may and ought to go out into the world cheerfully; and after doing all she can to make her situation, external and internal, and the situation of those around her, as happy as she can, she ought to study contentment. No circumstances, without this quality, can long confer happiness, or even cheerfulness; and with it, no ordinary circumstances, however unfavorable, can long render us miserable.

CHAPTER XXVI.

HABITS AND MANNERS.

Little things. Setting out in life. Important to set out right. Difficulty with some husbands. How to manage. Eugene and Juliet. General principles.

I HAVE more than once insisted, that the little things of life are, in their results, really the great and important things; and that it is therefore unwise to overlook them, as many are inclined to do. It is in the matrimonial state of life, however, that they are especially important. We cannot disregard them here, without doing it at our peril.

It will ever be the part of true friendship—and what is marriage worth without such an intimacy? —mutually to correct and reform each other. But by no friends can it be so well done as by husband and wife : first, because no relation is so intimate ; and secondly, because no friends have so good an opportunity of discovering each others' defects, in the smaller matters. Other friends see only a few of the larger failings; but in matrimony, unguarded as we are, all our smaller but more numerous defects are brought to light, and rendered susceptible of correction.

It is therefore of the utmost importance, that the parties should set out with a mutual determination to perform faithfully, and in a proper temper and spirit, the task of correcting one another's evil habits and manners. Let nothing, to this end, pass unnoticed. If you pass over a thing to-day, because it is slight, or because you feel a delicacy of mentioning it, remember you will pass over something else of at least equal—perhaps greater—importance to-morrow; and the next day, instead of one, you will omit two faults; the next day, three; and so on.

There are not a few husbands, whose general feelings are kind, and who will even engage in the work of mutual reformation with their whole hearts, who will, nevertheless, be greatly agitated, and sometimes, for the moment, almost angry, when certain things are mentioned to them as faults. They do not consider them worth minding; and sometimes, especially in the first moment of perturbation, will maintain that they are perfectly right.

With this sort of husbands, the young wife will be exceedingly tried. But let her not be surprised. Should impatience be manifested, at first, it will soon be regretted; and if they are conscientious men, they will not fail soon to acknowledge their error, and to accompany it with the proper marks of penitence. If they are without consciences, then indeed is your condition a sad one. Of those, however, who cannot be overcome by persevering kindness and faithfulness, the number is exceedingly small.

Eugene and Juliet entered into a mutual engagement of the kind here referred to, and faithfully pursued their respective tasks. But Eugene was sometimes irritable when told of a fault, and in some instances even complained; while Juliet continued immovable; and in his moments of perfect coolness, gently reminded him of his error. Ashamed of himself, he promised amendment; but his natural irritability of temper again and again overcame him. More than once did Juliet urge him to relinquish his engagement—but to no purpose. He was determined on reformation, and fully resolved on pursuing the means most likely to accomplish the object.

But it was not till after the lapse of six months or more, that he attained to the complete command of his temper, and could bear to be corrected in the minutest matters. However, perseverance at last succeeded, and a complete victory is now gained, of which he and his wife and the world are now reaping the benefits.

HABITS AND MANNERS.

To enumerate the thousand little errors of habit and manner to which we are liable, especially when we have been trained in the ordinary circumstances of New England families and schools, in which almost all these things are either overlooked or sacrificed to the hurry of business, is far from being my present intention. My main object was to lay down the principle, and leave each young wife to make the application. I will only observe that if you find habits of uncleanliness very prominent, do not be discouraged, but persevere with resolute kindness, hoping for final complete success. No one can know what may, in this way, be accomplished, till she has tried it. Remember that the removal of some bad habits, though they may seem trifling in themselves, is worth years of patient and untiring effort. Remember, too, that you are laboring, in these circumstances, not only for your husband and yourself, but for others, whose conduct and habits may and inevitably will be influenced, more or less, by your example.

CHAPTER XXVII.

DRESS.

Opinion of Paul. Real objects of dress. Modesty. Dress should regulate our temperature. Frequent change—why useful. General rule. A painful sight. Nature of profuse perspiration, or sweating. Material of dress. Objections to cotton. Fashion of dress. Compression of the lungs—its evils. Sympathies. Moderate indulgence. Hiding defects by dress. Dress of the husband.

On the subject of dress, Paul has some excellent remarks, in his epistles. While he does not condemn a proper regard to one's attire, he insists strongly on plainness and modesty; and inveighs against a fondness for ornaments. "I will," says he, "that women adorn themselves in modest apparel, with shame-facedness and sobriety; not with broidered hair, or gold, or pearls, or costly array, but with good works."

Never, perhaps, within the same compass, was better advice on this subject given to females—especially to married females. For if broidered hair and other ornaments were proper for any other individual, they are, at least, wholly unbecoming in a wife. She should be, above all, a model of simplicity, both in manners and in dress.

She should remember, first, the true objects of dress. To set off one's person is not, and never was, its primary object. Our dress is to cover us, to assist in regulating our temperature, to defend us from injuries, and to improve our appearance.

The mention of dress, as a means of improving our appearance, will no doubt be regarded, by many, as a full license to every indulgence, and every excess. But I mean not so much. Remember I do not place it first, but last, among the objects of dress. Nor does it follow, because I give it a place in the list—the last place—that any one is to be justified in inverting that order, and putting it at the head of the catalogue.

There are those who defeat, by its fashion, the first object for which dress was intended. Clothing, even in civilized life, does not always cover us. It sometimes leaves us partly uncovered; and this, too, not only in violation of every rule of common sense, but of the apostolic injunction—" I will that women adorn themselves in modest apparel."

I do not, of course, allude here to those violations of common sense and common decency, practised at this very time in our theatres, and countenanced, directly or indirectly, by some of those who consider themselves as sustaining, if not the first, at least an important station in society—violations which are a shame not only to our cities, but to our whole community—for with these, I hope and trust, few young wives will have anything to do. Their very presence and countenance would, in my view, be disgraceful to them. But I allude rather to those more common exposures of the chest and limbs which custom has sometimes tolerated, and which are even now sometimes practised, but which are no less improper than unhealthy.

Whatever others may or may not do, the young wife should set an example of the utmost regard to modesty in all her attire. As to the fashion, I shall not, of course, attempt to dictate. I suppose that there is a very wide range of fashion allowable, which is quite within the pale of modesty. The most refined or even fastidious French taste needs not, in any possible case, to pass its bounds.

The second grand object of dress is to regulate our temperature. I might perhaps say that its object is to increase our temperature—since it seldom if ever happens that our dress, in strictness of language, serves to cool us. In changing from a lower temperature to a higher one, as in passing from winter to summer, or even under the influence of a burning sun, one dress may be said to be cooler than another; but it is because it does not make us so hot as the other; or, in other words, it suffers the heat of our bodies to escape faster.

Hardly anything conduces more to our comfort, our eating and drinking perhaps excepted, than a due regard to the character and condition of our dress—especially in a climate so variable as ours. Many people suffer exceedingly, because they do not know how to regulate this matter, because they do not use the knowledge they possess, or because they imagine they cannot devote to it the necessary time.

Many an individual, of both sexes, will complain bitterly of the heat, when a little less clothing, or a dress a little lighter, would at once remove the whole cause of complaint. There seems to be a strange fear among us of the consequences of frequently changing our dress. Not a few suppose, or appear to suppose, that to go and change their dress, even on a midsummer day, will expose them to take cold. They will therefore continue to wear, through the day, whatever they happen to have put on in the morning, however hot or uncomfortable.

Now I am not ignorant that many persons, especially of my own sex, are either so situated or so employed, that a frequent change of dress, so as to meet the frequent changes of temperature in our variable climate, is impossible. But it is not for such that I am now writing. My remarks are directed to a class of persons who have, or might have it generally in their power to make changes, and who might exercise this power with entire safety.

It is true that without good sense, and the judicious use of it, the course I am recommending might expose a person to take cold. If the change of dress be too great, or if, on finding ourselves too hot, while at our labor, and our heat is increasing, we put on a thin dress, and then sit down, especially where there are cool currents of air circulating, we may and probably shall take cold. Or if we allow ourselves in making the exchange towards night, when we are much fatigued, or have, during the day, been much over-heated, we also endanger our safety.

But during the early part of the day, when we have neither been much fatigued in body or mind, nor much over-heated, there is no sort of danger in making any changes of dress we please, provided we continue our exercise after it; and provided, too, the change is not so great as to induce a degree of paleness, or a sensation of weakness, accompanied by a chill—which, however, under the restrictions I have here made, will not, so long as we are in health, often happen.

I dwell on this point the longer, because it is a point so intimately connected with the physical and mental comfort of every young housewife. How often have I seen this class of persons sweltering at midday, in full exercise, under a load of clothing which was not at all too great for the morning, but which, owing to certain whims in which they have been brought up, they dared not throw off.

If this were all, however—if the temporary inconvenience and suffering were the only suffering induced—there would be little comparative need that I should say anything on the subject. But this is very far from being the case. Every degree of this unnecessary heat and fatigue debilitates us, both in body and mind; and not only paves the way for, but actually sows the seeds of disease. And it is a matter which greatly needs to be corrected.

So important are the views which have been presented, to the comfort and health of those for whom they are intended, that I venture to repeat the rule. It is, that every housewife who is in good health, and in the use of moderate exercise, and who has not already become much fatigued or over-heated, may, with entire safety to health, change her dress, and to any extent she pleases, provided she does not go so far as to produce a chill. This last she must however guard against, and should therefore generally diminish her clothing very gradually.

There is, however, some degree of safety in changes which are sudden; but they require much care. A housewife who is in moderate exercise at the oven, or over the wash-tub, and not fatigued, might plunge into cold water, or use the shower bath. But it must be a mere plunge, or shower bath. She must not continue cold long. She must immediately resume her exercise, and secure a glow over the surface of the skin. This, however, is usually easy. If the glow or reaction could not be secured, she would inevitably be injured.

On the same principle it is that laborers in the field may, in the early part of a hot day, while little fatigued, safely plunge into a river, if they *only* plunge in, and come immediately out and go about their exercise, so as to secure, effectually, a reaction or glow on the surface of the body. No matter if the body is considerably heated at the time they plunge in, and if they are even perspiring pretty freely, if they only secure a reaction; for this is the main point. But if the hardiest person—even the savage—plunges in when greatly fatigued, or so much heated as to be weakened, or remains in the water too long, and does not secure a reaction when he comes out, but is pale, cold and feeble, and remains so, he is inevitably injured.

Let me not be misunderstood. I am not now recommending it to females to use the shower bath, or any form of cold bathing; but only endeavoring to illustrate my principle; for it is an important one. There is an immense amount of misery, both immediate and remote, produced to society by a neglect of it. On the subjects of bathing and cleanliness, I have, however, already said something in the chapter on Neatness.

I am sometimes inclined to think that one reason why the laboring portion of our community, especially females, are so frequently the subjects of disease, even in the most simple and healthful conditions of society, notwithstanding the healthy nature and tendency of their employments, in themselves considered, is that they over-heat their bodies so much. For it is an undeniable fact that, in the very healthiest parts of New England, in the most elevated country situations, where the diet and drink are comparatively good, and where mental causes of disease are comparatively inoperative, nearly every adult female is more or less diseased.

How many a time have I been pained at the sight of a healthy, vigorous housewife, torturing herself, and ruining her health—if not that of others—over a wash-tub, simply because she would not diminish the quantity or change the quality of her clothing. There she is, toiling and panting, with her face as red as if the blood would burst forth from its very surface. Yet she toils on, in hopes of speedy relief by means of a free perspiration. If she can only sweat freely, she tells us, she shall feel better.

No doubt she will. But it were far better to avoid the occasion for a violent perspiration. It does no one any good; nay, it weakens everybody. I do not say that it is not useful, as a choice of evils. If a housewife will heat herself to excess, it is a wise and merciful provision of her heavenly Father, that she can get rid of a part of the evil consequences, by a profuse perspiration. This is the substitution of a lesser evil to prevent a greater.

Let me not be understood as saying that everything beyond what is commonly called an insensible perspiration, is injurious. As things are, it is not so. We are in the daily if not hourly use of so many causes of unnecessary heat, external and internal, that, did not excessive or profuse perspiration occasionally come on to relieve us, at least partially, we should be destroyed much sooner than we actually are. Our mental anxieties, our cares, our perplexities, our improper passions, our exciting and stimulating food and drink, our hot rooms, and a thousand other things, are continually heating us beyond what nature intended. This makes it the more necessary that I should press the importance of not adding to the general conflagration by unnecessary clothing, but rather that we should use the least amount of clothing which is compatible with comfort.

But prone as we are to extremes, equal care should be taken not to use, on the contrary, too little clothing. This is injurious, though perhaps less so than too much. A want of suitable clothing is only a steady source of chronic disease, especially if we are trained to it; but the heat which is induced by an excess of clothing not only favors the direct production of many diseases, both acute and chronic, particularly bilious complaints, but by rendering us tender, weakens all our organs, and prepares them for other diseases, and then exposes us to colds, which excite them.

True wisdom, in regard to dress, consists in so educating the body, from the first, that only a small amount of clothing is required. Possibly one good suit of firm and appropriate clothing might, in such circumstances, and in this climate, be sufficient. But as we now are, at twenty, thirty, fifty years of age, accustomed to a great deal of clothing, both in summer and winter, a reduction, at once, to this amount, would not only be uncomfortable, but in some instances, and with some states of constitution, quite unsafe. I will only say that in hot weather, we generally use far too much; and that the use of too much clothing, at any season and under any circumstances, is very greatly injurious.

I lay it down, then, as a general rule, that while we should never yield, one moment, to the mistaken, but very prevalent notion, that going cold hardens us,* we should always keep as cool as we can, without being uncomfortable. One degree of unnecessary heat is more injurious than two of unnecessary cold.

In regard to the material of dress, I have little to say. For summer, especially midsummer, I prefer linen; for winter, flannel. For warm, damp days, silk next to the skin would often be useful, because it is so bad a conductor of electricity, and would save many of those unpleasant sensations which we feel, when we call the air thick and heavy. The damp air, in these circumstances, conducts away from our bodies too much of the electricity; and this is probably one source of our bad feelings.

---

* Going cold may, indeed, slightly harden us, but not without too great a sacrifice of our original stock of vital power. It is not, therefore, safe to attempt any such hardening process—certain savage nations to the contrary notwithstanding.

I prefer linen in summer, and flannel in winter, to the entire exclusion of cotton—chiefly because so many accidents result from the use of the latter. Hundreds lose their lives every year, in consequence of fire communicated to their cotton clothing. Greater care would indeed save many of the number; but it would be difficult for the housewife always to keep away from the fire; and therefore it is my advice that she keep away from the use of cotton, at least in any way that shall expose it to take fire.

In regard to the fashion of female dress, it is sufficient to observe that it should always be loose and flowing, and without ligatures of any sort. The evils of dressing tightly are numerous, and some of them serious in their consequences.

As a general fact, any part of the dress, worn tightly, obstructs the circulation. This should always be free. The consequences of tight caps, bonnets, &c., to the adult, are less injurious than those of any other tight dress, because the pressure does not much affect the tender brain, enclosed as it is in a thick bony case. They keep the head too hot, it is true; but even this is not so serious an evil to a grown person as it is to a child.

But the compression of almost any other part of the adult system is more serious in its consequences. Compression of the hands or feet, besides obstructing the circulation, and rendering them cold, and producing, on the feet, what are called corns, prevents their sending out healthy sympathies to other parts. It is a law of the human frame, from which even the hands and feet are not exempt, that if one member or part suffers, all the rest suffer with it; and that if one member rejoices, all the other members rejoice with it. That is to say, if the hands or feet are in a good, sound, healthful condition—rejoicing, as one might term it—they send out, as it were, their messengers of joy to all other parts, and these rejoice—become more sound, vigorous and healthy, along with them. This is, I say, true of the hands and feet; though it is much more true of the lungs, stomach, liver, heart, brain, &c.

Compression of the neck is also injurious; but to this evil, females at the present time, and with the present fashions, seem not much exposed. Compression of the lower limbs is more common and more injurious. Besides rendering the legs and feet cold, the use of any sort of ligature below the knee exposes a person to what are called varicose veins, which sometimes prove exceedingly troublesome, and baffle the skill of the most eminent surgeons. I have known instances where these varicose veins became so enlarged as finally to break forth and form ulcers as lasting as life.

Of all forms or modes of compressing the human structure, the worst, however, is the fashionable custom of compressing the lungs. These are so well enclosed by bone, that no ordinary pressure produces immediate sensible evil; and yet the bones, on three sides, are so yielding and disengaged, that even moderate pressure, if continued for a long time, diminishes the space they have to move in; that is, diminishes what is called the cavity of the chest, where the lungs are situated.

It is in this view that nearly every medical writer, who has any knowledge of anatomy and physiology, has protested against every form of tight lacing the chest. Indeed, it seems impossible that any individual who understands its structure can doubt on this point. And yet a few do. Dr. Dunglison, in his "Elements of Hygiene," and Dr. Sweetser, in his work on "Consumption," both attribute the evils of tight lacing by stays, corsets, &c., to *excess* in the use of them; while they more than intimate, especially Dr. D., that moderate pressure on the chest and abdomen is, in some persons, useful.

I was not at all surprised that Mrs. Phelps, in her "Female Student," should defend a moderately tight dress. Nor is it strange that Dr. Dunglison, who defends the moderate use of poisonous drinks, should also justify the moderate use of a worse than poisonous dress. Yet I was not prepared, I confess, to hear similar sentiments avowed by the excellent and learned Dr. Sweetser.

But they are certainly mistaken, and, I trust, will not long attempt to stand it out against nearly the whole medical and scientific world. It is impossible for a considerate person—so it appears to me—to believe that the great Creator would have left the fore part of the human frame so weak as to require, in the healthy person, a constant artificial bracing.

And what seems so unlikely, we may be fully assured, has never, in point of fact, happened. Every ounce of pressure beyond the weight of our clothing is, if long continued, injurious. It is injurious, first, just as a weight hung to a door is injurious, by causing it to open and close with more difficulty, and thus producing unnecessary wear. Secondly, it is injurious by causing an unnecessary expenditure of vitality, in our constant efforts to support, like a burdened saddle horse, the unnecessary weight. Thirdly, the want of action favors, and even invites disease. Fourthly, it prevents the full and free circulation of air, and the consequent change of the impure blood which is sent into the lungs; and fifthly, it does great mischief by sending out to all other organs and parts of the body, its unhealthy sympathies.

These five positions against tight dress of any kind, for the lungs, appear to me so plain, so obvious, and so well established by modern writers, that I hardly need to attempt their elucidation. We have probably all heard how the inactivity of the lungs favors or invites inflammation of those organs, and consequent colds, asthmas, lung fevers and consumptions; and we all know that mischief must follow, whenever the impure, black blood of the human system cannot be effectually purified in the cavity of the lungs, whither it is sent for that special purpose.

There is, however, one point on which it is necessary for me to dwell a few moments, because other writers, though they have not always wholly omitted it, have not attached to it, as it seems to me, sufficient importance. I allude to the unhealthy sympathies which are extended by the lungs, when unduly compressed.

The sympathy of the lungs with other organs is not always in proportion to their nearness, but rather to their relative concernment in the same office. Thus the skin, which fulfils, in part, the same office with the lungs, has the most powerful, striking, and important sympathies with those organs. Hence it is that when the lungs are compressed, the skin, though it may seem for a while to make increased effort, is at last enfeebled, and being unable to do its part in the general work of purifying the blood and other fluids of the system, it becomes pale, flaccid, loose or shrunk, and diseased.

It should also be remembered that the moment the skin begins to suffer, this, too, extends its sympathies, unhealthy and diseased as they are, not only back to the lungs, but to all other parts of the body, especially the lining membrane of the intestines. These again, in their turn, react both on the skin and the lungs; and if there were no redeeming circumstances to interpose, the whole system, in its multifarious parts and organs, would be involved in a sort of civil war, which would continue till the system itself was destroyed.

Do you say this is a frightful picture? Frightful as it is, I cannot doubt that the reality, could you behold it, would be still more so—much, I say, more so, because it is not the skin alone on which fall the first evil impressions or sympathetic actions. Other organs immediately suffer, some more, others less; and all in proportion to the degree and permanence of the pressure, and their relation to the parts which first feel the evils of the compression.

It would be well if the mischief which ensues ended with the sufferer. But alas! as a general rule, it is not so. It only begins with her. Its effects go on to generations that come after her. If, in the progress of the world's history, she should have thousands of descendants, not one of them, to the remotest periods of time, would be precisely what he might have been, had she conformed more strictly to the natural laws—the laws of the human constitution.

These may be hard sayings, but hard as they are, they must not be suppressed. The whole truth must be told. If people will destroy themselves and those who come after them, they ought not, at least, to be suffered to do it blindly. Let their eyes be opened, and the truth be faithfully told and reiterated, and then, if there should be found among us those who will not give heed to the truth, who shall say that public sentiment ought not, in strict justice, to be turned against them?

I am not ignorant that every young wife will plead her own innocence in this matter of tight dressing. *She* knows, she says, full well, the abominable evils of the practice; and, for herself, never dresses so tightly as to produce the least possible injury. Other people do, she is well aware, but she wonders at their folly, and always did.

Now I repeat the sentiment; that if a moderate indulgence in this practice be admitted, the practice itself can never be suppressed. For every one will plead that, for her own part, she keeps quite within the bounds of a reasonable moderation; so that no transgressors, by confession, can be found. The worst—they who are dying—are always among the *moderates;* and they pity most heartily those who approach even the borders.

A young lady in ——, besides wearing corsets very tight, is accustomed to fasten her dress around her so closely as to require the main strength of an assistant to bring it together. Yet no one, more than she, pities those who are addicted to the foolish habit of tight lacing. She wonders they can do it. She, for her part, wears her clothes very loose indeed; she would not dress tightly for the world.

I have said elsewhere, that every ounce weight of pressure, beyond the weight of the clothes, is injurious; and I have no disposition to recall the sentiment. It must be reiterated and believed. To dress in entire accordance with the best interests of our frame, would be, as Mr. Dick, in one of his recent works, has justly observed, to let our clothes hang loosely from our shoulders. Certain it is—and I repeat it once for all—that all compression about the chest of either sex, especially of females, is more or less injurious, and must, in the progress of human improvement, be abandoned.

And now, after all that I have said, I have little hope of accomplishing much good. People are so wedded to long established customs, and so enslaved to fashion, that there is very little hope of leading them into a "more excellent way." There is, however, one ray of hope for our encouragement. Though the young wife may not have moral courage to abandon tight dressing herself, she may have courage, so far as she has absolute control over others, to prevent their following her example. It is true, her own example will be in the way of her lessons, but something can be done in spite of it.

People who have been accustomed to brace the chest, feel not only a degree of uneasiness, but an actual want of their usual strength, if the support is at once discontinued. Hence they infer its necessity to themselves, trained as they are, though they may deny its necessity to others. But the dram drinker, or opium, or snuff, or tobacco taker, or tea or coffee drinker, might plead for indulgence, on the same principle that people plead for corsets. They, too, feel a loss of strength, as if they should fall to pieces, if they do not have their accustomed support. And she who will not lay aside her corsets, because she shall have bad feelings if she does, must not be found complaining of others, if they refuse, for precisely the same reason, to lay aside their spirits, their wine, their cider, their beer, their tobacco, their opium, their tea and their coffee.

I have said something of dress, as a means of improving our appearance; but before I close this chapter, I wish to say a few words on its use as a means of concealing personal deformities.

When we look at a person who is deformed, our eye, almost involuntarily, first catches the deformity. This naturally embarrasses—sometimes pains him; and at second thought, perhaps, we perceive the evil we have done, and wish we had avoided it. I do not say it is not a mark of impoliteness thus to gaze at the deformities of a stranger;—be it so. Still it is a very common case, and will be likely to continue so.

When, therefore, I approve of using dress to conceal deformities of person, it is in reference to these known traits of human nature. It is to prevent giving or receiving pain, and establishing those unfavorable first impressions which it is so difficult afterwards to eradicate. I am far from intending to give license, by my remarks, to anything which even approaches the borders of foppery in dress, or even of gaiety.

I like, I confess, to see a young wife neatly dressed. There is a neatness which is perfectly compatible with plainness; and a dress may be graceful, without being ridiculous. I love, in this respect, simplicity; I can bear a degree of gaiety; but I cannot endure levity.

I like a neat simplicity, because, somehow or other, there appears to be a frequent connection between the outside and the inside. The exterior is, to some extent, a key to the interior. If I see a person dressed like a thorough-going fop, I cannot, if I would, respect the mind of that person. Even where a future close acquaintance discloses to me my error, it is hard to overcome first impressions.

When I first saw the picture of Mrs. Hemans, the friend who directed me to it concealed, for a time, the name, and asked me how I liked it. Accustomed as I was to look with pain, and sometimes with horror, on a human being shaped like a wasp, I told him frankly I did not like it very well. He was surprised; he thought it the most perfect thing of the kind he had ever seen, &c. I, too, was surprised, when I found whose picture it was; and I have little doubt that it would have altered, to some extent, my opinion, had I known beforehand to whom it belonged. Still, under any circumstances whatever, such a wasp-like waist would lower my estimate of the good sense of the person to whom it belonged.

A wife, I have said, should dress neatly, though plainly. It is a duty which she owes to the community. It is a duty to her husband. It is a duty to the rest of her household, if she have any.

It is a duty to herself. Let her study, however, to avoid pernicious fashions.

A person who has no regard for her own appearance, will be apt to overlook the appearance of her husband. This will be of less consequence, if he have wealth. The wealthy and influential can better afford to disregard their dress, since they will seldom lose anything by it. Not so with the poor man. He cannot afford to neglect his exterior. His coat must not only be in good style, but must be kept properly and neatly mended.

I have seen females who neglected all the latter sort of work;—wives they were called, but they were unworthy of the name. They were by no means going to stoop to the paltry business of mending garments. Though willing their husband should appear well, they were more willing to let his elbow protrude through a hole in the sleeve.

The good wife deems nothing which tends to health, comfort, or true respectability, beneath her notice. She can not only make a loaf of bread, (for that is the summit of the art of cookery,) and a good pudding, but she can mend clothes, and darn stockings. In one word, she regards nothing as mean which she believes to be duty.

CHAPTER XXVIII.

HEALTH.

Purity of the air in our apartments. Purity of clothing—furniture—cellars—drains—wells, &c. Personal cleanliness. Its expense not to be considered. Various modes of exercise. Household labor. Exercise in the open air. Walking. Riding. Health, in our own keeping. Health of the husband. General remarks.

ALTHOUGH several chapters in other parts of this work, especially those on Economy and Neatness, treat of health in many important points, yet I should leave my plan in a very unfinished state, if I should neglect to mention, under a general head, a few particulars which are not included elsewhere. The subject of bodily health, in itself, but more especially in reference to its connection with mental health, is of too much consequence to the class of persons for whom this book is designed, to be lightly passed over.

And first, let me speak of the purity of the air in our apartments. Need I remind my reader that there are a thousand substances connected with every kitchen, which should be speedily removed, or they may be a means of producing disease? Does she not know enough of chemistry to induce her to prevent, to the utmost of her power, the accumulation of any other gas, within her precincts, than that mixture of oxygen and nitrogen—the atmosphere—which has been prepared for our use by the Creator?

Whether carpets render the air impure, to an extent which favors the production of pulmonary diseases, as some German writer has recently told us, I am not certain. But the known facts that they entangle and retain with readiness much bad air, and that they often prove an excuse for neglect of sweeping and washing our rooms, should lead us to doubt, very much, their general utility.

But whether carpets be used or not, the utmost pains should be taken by every young housewife—and the sooner she forms the habit, the better—to keep the floor and the walls of every room perfectly clean, and the air perfectly sweet. To this end, all rooms should be frequently aired. All clothing, whether it be wearing apparel or bed clothing, should be frequently shaken well and exposed; and the more frequently, in proportion to the warmth and moisture of the surrounding atmosphere. Beds, whether slept in or not, but especially if used, should be often thrown open, and duly exposed to pure air.

All furniture, large or small, should be constantly watched, and kept perfectly sweet and clean. There should be no putting away the implements of eating and drinking, in such a state as to render the things themselves acid or impure, or the air around them unfit for healthy respiration. I speak now of a healthy state of a family. In sickness, the caution is more important still.

I have seen families accounted perfectly neat, who yet suffered so many things to spoil in the house, that I wondered not, on the appearance of an epidemic disease, to see it break in upon them, and carry off from three to six of their number. I have said they were accounted neat; but were they truly so? Look at the cellars, the kitchens, the drains, and the yards! See the putrefied vegetables and fluids, the half spoiled meat, the offal matter, the heaps of manure, the vaults! See the well, with which it is ten to one but some of these communicate, but which, perhaps, has not been cleansed for four or five years!

You will say that all this belongs to the husband, rather than the housewife. Granted it were so, it can do no harm to remind the housewife of it, that she may remind him. He is busy here and there, and may overlook it; but the organs of sight and smell, of those who are hourly annoyed, will not so readily permit this. It is not, however, true that the matter belongs exclusively to the husband. It belongs to both. God has established the institution of matrimony, in part, for the mutual education of the parties; and a due attention to each other's health is a most important portion of the great work. Besides, reason as we will, all these things are attended to or neglected, according to the housewife's estimate of their importance.

But personal cleanliness is not less important, in this respect, than the cleanliness of our dwellings, and everything around them. The young wife must not only sustain the husband's efforts, as far as he seems inclined to go, but even urge him on. There is not one husband in a hundred who will not need this assistance. There is not one in a hundred who, notwithstanding his neatness, or rather particularity, in some points, will not find his health and happiness essentially promoted by giving heed to the promptings of a judicious companion, in matters pertaining both to purity of person and clothing.

The truth is, that females make discoveries that their husbands are very apt to overlook. They see the smallest specks of dirt; and observe the tendencies to negligence, in their most incipient state. They may not, indeed, without instruction, understand to the full extent their bearing on health; but they know, full well, that all is not right; and wo to the husband who despises their suggestions and counsels, merely because he cannot count their worth in dollars and cents.

It is not my purpose to enter deeply, here, into particulars. Indeed, in regard to dress, I cannot; and my readers must not expect it. In regard to cleanliness of person, a few remarks may be of some service.

The importance of local washings—of the hands, face, neck, feet, &c.—is generally conceded. I do not say it is generally practised; for half the work of this kind which is done, is only half done. Multitudes of busy as well as fastidiously delicate people, instead of washing themselves, do little more than to make a mockery of it. To wash is to make clean, and not merely to make believe we have made clean. But I have said enough on this point, under the head of Neatness.

Perhaps I ought, however, to say something of the *manner* of performing our ablutions. This may be either with simple water or with soap and water; the temperature of the water may be high or low; and the mode of application extensively various. There is the cold bath, the warm bath, the hot bath, and the vapor bath; and either of these may be simple or medicated. I am not, however, now prescribing for the sick, and must therefore omit all further notice of baths which are medicated. The cold bath may be applied by the sponge or the hand, in the form of a simple washing, in the form of the shower bath, or in the form of submersion or plunging. For the mere purpose of cleansing the surface, it makes little difference which of these modes is adopted; but when we wish to combine with the purposes of cleanliness, an increase of bodily tone and vigor, the shower bath may be, perhaps, as effectual as any. The simple washing of the surface with the hand is most convenient; but this may and should be appended to the shower bath.

The cold bath is best in the early part of the day, when we have enough vigor of constitution to secure a reaction, which is the case much oftener than is usually supposed. By beginning with water which is but moderately cold, or by going at first quickly through with the process, there are few persons who are not actually sick, who cannot soon learn to endure it, and even find it a luxury. I have known whole families, some of whose members were far from being very vigorous, begin the practice of daily cold bathing in midwinter, and without the least inconvenience. Indeed, I believe it will generally be found that water of a temperature at least as low as 45 degrees, is more comfortable, or at least more likely to be followed by a glow, than that which is of a higher temperature.

Do you say the practice requires time and expense? As to the expense, in money, it is not worth considering. How much does it cost, to erect apparatus enough for shower bathing? How much to get a bathing tub? How much to provide even for warm or vapor bathing? And as to time, even, how easy is it to redeem, from that abominable waste of this most precious gift of God which everywhere prevails, in unnecessary cookery, an ample supply, not only to bathe once, but, were it necessary, ten times a day.

But exercise is nearly as necessary to every housewife as purity of air, and cleanliness of person and clothing. This, however, she who dispenses with servants will be very likely to procure. This was, in fact, one object which I had in view, when I insisted that females ought to do their own work.—Were it not accounted, by many, as rank heresy, I might insist strongly, as I have done elsewhere, that nearly every female would be benefited by moderate agricultural or horticultural labor.

Nothing short of the actual performance of the usual labors of the kitchen will, however, secure and preserve the health of the young wife. Without this, at least, she will almost inevitably suffer.

If proof were necessary in the case, we might find it in the actual condition of this class of the community—diseased, most of them, more or less, for want of suitable exercise; and this before they are twenty-five, or at most, thirty years of age.

There are, however, other forms of exercise which will serve as partial substitutes for house work. Among the more important of these is walking. She who dares not venture to be so singular as to work in the garden or in the field, and is yet too proud to labor in the house, may preserve her health, in some good measure, by walking.

Some females cannot walk, they tell us. And they say this, no doubt, in sincerity. Much depends on habit. Some who are constitutionally vigorous, and can perform a great deal of in-door labor, soon tire, if they attempt to walk. But the reason is, they have never been accustomed to it. Let them begin by walking a short distance at a time, and they will soon find themselves able to walk several miles at once, with as much ease as they could at first a quarter of a mile. I have seen experiments of this sort so frequently made, that I feel fully confident I have not exaggerated.

But the ability to walk, valuable as it is in itself, is not the only thing gained by the exercise. The whole system is invigorated at the same time; and the mind, too, is a gainer with the rest. To what extent the physical and mental constitution may be improved by out-of-door exercises—moderate labor, walking and riding—I am unable to determine.

Riding on horseback, next to walking, is the most salutary exercise for females, in the open air. The lighter games, as battledore, hook and ring, &c., are of little comparative value. I will not say that they are entirely useless, but compared with household work and walking, they seem scarcely worthy of being mentioned.

Those who recommend active exercise to females, and to those of the other sex who lead a sedentary life, appear, in their directions, to aim no higher than the preservation of what vigor they at present enjoy. The idea of adding to the stock of a person's health, between the ages of twenty and forty, seems scarcely to be thought of. It will, however, be seen, by the foregoing remarks, however heterodox the opinion may be, that I fondly cherish it. I believe it to be the duty of every individual, to improve in bodily and mental strength and activity, till thirty-five or forty years of age. There may indeed be a few exceptions to such a rule, but I think they are exceedingly rare.

One thing is certain—and were we sure of nothing more, the object would be worthy of our highest efforts—that our health is, as a general rule, committed, by a wise and glorious Creator, to our own keeping. We are, under God, as much the artificers of physical as of moral character. Both are attainable upon the same general condition, viz., EFFORT, or ACTION. To prevent corporeal illness, says Dr. Johnson, in his "Economy of Health," as well as to prevent that state of mind which usually attends it, we must "keep the body active, and the stomach empty." Not that even Dr. J. would have us over-act, on the one hand, or starve, on the other; but he well knew the effects of incessant action, when not immoderate. We should feel as if we had no time to be sick.

I might dwell, at considerable length, on the importance of every individual virtue of the whole catalogue, in promoting health and happiness; especially of the salutary tendency, not only of temperance, bodily and mental, in every form, but of cheerfulness, hope, and especially faith. The truth is, there is not a single quality which improves, adorns or exalts us, as social, intellectual, political, moral or religious beings, which will not at the same time benefit our health. Nor is it less true that, philosophically speaking, every particle we gain of physical vigor adds something to the stock of intellect and morality. It is in this view, and with these sentiments, that I so frequently suffer one chapter to run into and trench upon another. Such is the connection which I plainly perceive between health and morals, that I scarcely know how to separate them.

One word more. The wife should never forget, in any of her movements, that she is responsible, in no small degree, for the health of her husband, no less than of herself. None of us, says the Bible, liveth to himself, and none of us dieth to himself; and if this remark is peculiarly applicable in any relation of life short of that of brethren in the church, it is in matrimony. A great deal might be written—nay, a great deal has been written—to point out the proper means and methods in which and by which woman may discharge some of her relative duties. Enough for me, however, in this place, if I endeavor to see that she do not lose sight of her own happiness and that of her husband.

But it would require volumes to present, in detail, all the rules and directions which might properly be presented, in relation to the means of preserving and improving health. It would be to enter deeply into the philosophy of the human frame, in all its parts and functions, and to speak at length of exercise, temperature, air, sleep and dietetics. So closely, indeed, is our physical well-being dependent on the quantity and character of our food, that this alone requires a volume. All I can do in a work like the present, and, I trust, all that will be expected, will be, that I should barely allude to the subject. Of the importance of study, and of the instruments by which a course of study is to be pursued, I propose to say something in another place.

CHAPTER XXIX.

ATTENDING THE SICK

Attending the sick should be a part of female education. Objections to this view considered. Reasons why females should be thus trained. Their native qualifications for this office. Their labor cheaper. They have stronger sympathies. Application of the principle to the case of the young wife.

THAT system of female education is wholly incomplete, which leaves neglected the art of nursing the sick. If it should be said that on this principle we have no perfect system of female education, I shall not object to the inference, nor attempt to lessen its force. I have long held, and still hold, the opinion, that every female should be taught the art of ministering at our bedside, and " binding the brow " in pain and in sickness.

The greatest known objection to this principle is, that it is sounder economy to expend our efforts in the way of preventing evil to the rising generation, in our own families and elsewhere, than to employ any large portions of our time in the correction of evils which have already arisen.

This objection would have more force, if the art of managing the sick required the expenditure of much time; but it does not. If we make the most in our power of the occurrences of life, in our own families and in the families of those around us, there is little danger that females will very soon be in want of opportunities for informing themselves in the art of attending the sick. I am as solicitous that we should be ready to serve our fellow beings, out of our own families, in cases of sickness, as I am that we should withhold our service and refuse that of our neighbors, in other circumstances.

The truth is, that as the world now is, every neighborhood of much size has, every year, if not almost every month, a greater or less amount of sickness. Sometimes the disease is slight, at others it is more severe. The art of rendering all our young ladies proper attendants on the sick consists in employing them whenever any sickness occurs, instead of requiring them, as is now the case almost universally, to stand at a distance.

"But shall we not, in this way, expose their health?" it may be asked. Expose their health! How? "Why, it always exposes our health to go among the sick," I shall be told. Not so fast, however. A little explanation is necessary.

It exposes our health to do anything beyond our strength, whether among the sick or the well. But in the ordinary circumstances of disease, there is no necessity that a female should go beyond her strength. Indeed, one prominent object of educating all females to the art of attending the sick is to prevent this. When there is only an individual here and there—one perhaps in a family, or sometimes only one in a neighborhood—that "understands sickness," as it is called, the danger of going beyond the strength is often considerable. But where every wife and daughter is equally qualified for the task, there is no necessity of the kind. Every hour of laborious employment can be alternated with several hours of relief or relaxation.

"But is it not true," you will perhaps ask, "that the sick room itself endangers the health, let our presence in it be ever so short?" Yes, it does, if there is a contagious disease, or if the room and its contents are not often enough ventilated. But contagion, in the usual acceptation of the term, is seldom present; and when it is, the danger of being affected by it is greatly heightened by our fears of it, and by the want of confidence or courage which those who are newly initiated into the mysteries of the sick room almost always feel, and still more, by that over-fatigue to which, in the existing state of things, they are almost always subjected. Old nurses and attendants of the sick, and physicians, seldom contract disease; and one reason is, they have no fears of doing so. Some of these may be found in such places as New York and Philadelphia, who are quite aged, and yet have spent their lives, as it were, in the sick room, even amid what is usually regarded as contagion.

It is not indeed contended that the young girl of only six or eight years of age, who has never been present where a person was sick enough to be confined to his bed, ought to be plunged at once into the midst of fever or cholera. Let young girls, from the earliest age at which they can possibly be of service, be accustomed gradually to the sick room; first, where the disease is mild—perhaps little more than a cold; and afterward, where it exists in its severer forms. If the exposure is thus gradual, they will seldom know what the fear of disease is; and thus escape pain, when there is no occasion for it, and danger, when danger actually exists.

This general reasoning on the subject would have less force, if the education or training to which I have referred was costly, or difficult of access. But it is not so. Not that all which is valuable of the most liberal education afforded by the best schools in the world, would not be useful to one who was to spend her days as a female attendant of the sick; doubtless it would. Still, so liberal an education will not, for many centuries to come, if ever, be attainable by the mass of our female population; nor is it wholly indispensable. A good common school education, including, as every common school education should, a tolerable knowledge of chemistry, botany, anatomy and physiology, joined to that gradual introduction to the sick room and its inmates of which I have already spoken, would render young females, in general, as well qualified attendants as the best now are—and probably more so.

Thus have I shown that the objections which are commonly brought against this part of what I call an appropriate female education, have very little weight. I now proceed to show, in greater detail, the reasons for what I propose.

It sometimes happens that here and there a female in single life is unemployed. To such persons, nursing or attending the sick would be a sort of profession, not only highly beneficial to mankind, but profitable to themselves. It is a common saying, that "a good nurse is worth as much to the sick patient as a physician;" and there is no little truth in it. And since it is so, and since females are better adapted to the performance of this task than males, it is of the highest importance to the former, in particular, that they should be instructed in it. No individual would, in my view, lose anything by it, while not a few in society would not only be saved from ennui, or disgust with life, but rendered happy in themselves, and a source of happiness to those around them.

Females are better calculated, by nature and providence, for attending the sick, than males. They have more fortitude in scenes of trial and distress; their manners and methods are more gentle; their devotion to what they undertake is greater; their thoughts less engrossed by other objects, especially the cares and pressure of business; and, what would seem to follow, their attention is more constant and unremitted. In a word, they are formed for days, and nights, and months, and years of watchfulness, not only over our infancy, but over both our first and second childhood; and it were strange indeed if the Creator, in qualifying them for all this, had not also qualified them to watch over us and bind our brow, in the pain and sickness of the years that intervene.

It is true that there are cases which require the aid, if not the constant presence, of an assistant, whose physical strength is greater than that of most females; but even in these cases, the services of the female attendant are most important and most indispensable.

Female attendance, where it is to be paid for, can of course be afforded much cheaper than that of the other sex. This, to a community like ours, is a consideration of importance. It is also an object of great importance—and to the lower class, no less than to the higher—that the same attendant or set of attendants should be secured to the same individual, during his whole sickness. So much mischief is done in the world by constantly changing the responsibility, in these cases, that I have for years insisted, and must continue to insist, on the importance of regular attendance. This is an additional reason for the employment, and consequently, for the education of females with reference to this point.

Once more. Females sympathize with the sick more than males, and by consequence, anticipate more readily their wants. I was struck, once, with the remark of a friend who, having just been sick, was comparing two of his attendants. "A.," said he, "did well; but B. did better. A. brought everything as soon as I asked for it, but B. a little before."

To apply the foregoing remarks to the case of the young wife—In a world like this, she cannot expect to escape scenes of distress and sickness. Some member of her family will sooner or later be likely to demand attendance. Is it her husband?

Will she be willing to leave him wholly to the care of others? Will she not pass many—perhaps the most—of the tedious hours at his bedside?

How happy will it now be for both parties, if she have been educated to her task! How happy if her feelings do not overcome her better judgment, and lead her to destroy, in circumstances to which she may be brought, the very individual whom she would give the world to save!

CHAPTER XXX.

LOVE OF INFANCY AND CHILDHOOD.

What the love of childhood is. Frequent want of it. Dr. Gregory's opinion—Mr. Addison's. Great gulf fixed between children and adults. Love of childhood favorable to mental improvement—to the happiness of the wife—to the happiness of her husband—to religious improvement. Example of the Saviour. How to elicit this love, when it is wanting. Remarks on faith, and its importance. What faith can enable us to accomplish.

It may strike some readers as singular, that I should lay it down as a duty of the young wife, to cultivate a love of infancy and childhood. Every one loves children, it will be said, and when such a love is wanting, all the rules in the world for developing or cultivating it will do no good.

But it is not true that all persons have a genuine love of infancy and childhood. A person may have a sort of instinctive love of children, because they happen to be her own relatives or friends, without a particle of that feeling to which I now refer—the love of infancy and childhood for its own sake. Perhaps this trait might be included under the word *simplicity*, taken in its largest sense; but it is so prominent and so important a trait of human character, that it seems best to devote to its consideration a separate chapter.

The love of infancy and childhood leads us to take an interest in the things which delight and interest children. And however we may explain the fact, or whether it is at all explicable or not, we believe nothing is better proved than that the free intercourse of the old with the young greatly conduces to the health and longevity of the former. We cannot stop to fortify, by authority, all of what may be deemed our *heresies*, but the following remarks, from the distinguished Dr. Gregory, of Edinburgh, are too important to be unnoticed, especially on a point which is so universally overlooked or disregarded.

"Old people would find great advantage in associating rather with the young than with those of their own age. The conversation of young people dissipates their gloom, and communicates a cheerfulness, and something else, perhaps, which we do not fully understand, of great consequence to health and the prolongation of life. There is a universal principle of imitation among mankind, which disposes them to catch instantaneously, and without being conscious of it, the resemblance of any action or character that presents itself. We have numberless examples of this, in the similitude of character and manners induced by people living much together. We will not attempt to explain the nature of this mental infection; but it is a fact well established that such a thing exists, and that there is such a thing in nature as a healthy sympathy, as well as a morbid infection.

"An old man, who enters into this philosophy, is far from envying, or proving a check on the innocent pleasures of young people, and particularly of his own children. On the contrary, he attends with delight to the gradual opening of the imagination, and the dawn of reason; he enters, by a secret sort of sympathy, into their guiltless joys, that revive in his memory the tender images of his youth, which, as Mr. Addison observes, by length of time, have contracted a softness inexpressibly agreeable; and thus the evening of life is protracted to a happy, honorable and unenvied old age."

Nor is familiar intercourse with the young much less conducive to the health and happiness of persons in middle age. It is recommended, therefore, to every young wife, to interest herself as much as may be, in the amusements, employments and conversation of children. Or if she is naturally inclined to do so, she will do well to preserve assiduously the habit.

I have been surprised at the difference of mankind, in regard to the point in question. Some very excellent people never appear to have the least possible sympathy with infancy and childhood. Indeed, children seldom approach them in a free, familiar manner; or if they do, they seem to discover, as if by instinct, their disposition, and soon make their retreat.

It is a most unfortunate circumstance, that fashion, and custom, and business, have fixed such a great gulf between children and adults, and especially between children and the aged. Children live in the future, and naturally—I had almost said instinctively—delight in hearing the conversation and stories of those who are older. And yet the latter, who live in the past, and delight as much in relating what they have seen and heard as children do in hearing it, seem, for the most part, to stand aloof from them, and even to bury this fund of instruction in the grave of their decaying faculties. Why is this gulf of separation kept up, to the great loss of all parties and of the world? Let us be grateful to Heaven that attempts are beginning to be made to pass it, the results of which cannot be otherwise than successful and happy.

The love of juvenile character which I recommend is greatly conducive to intellectual improvement. Those who associate much with children seem to make far greater mental progress than persons in other circumstances. "Teaching we learn, and giving we retain;" and it is scarcely possible to be much with the young, without falling into the habit of instructing them. And this habit of hearing and answering infantile and juvenile questions, is highly favorable to the development of our own minds. It is so when all we do for them is in the way of story telling. The single habit of telling stories to the young—especially of striving to excel in it—with a view to gain their attention, and please and interest them, is of great value.

This disposition conduces greatly, in a young wife, to her own happiness. The young instinctively love, and ultimately respect those who sympathize with and love them—those to whom they can go when they please, with all the freedom and frankness with which they approach their playmates. And as they grow up into the world, their respect for such elder friends continues and increases. But is it not a source of happiness to an individual, to find herself surrounded by a rising generation who all esteem and love her?

Must not this state of things also greatly interest and contribute to the happiness of the husband? Can he see the companion of his choice gaining in vigor and elasticity of body and mind, and securing the love and confidence of those around her, without being himself made happier? Nay, more; what husband is there in the world, who is one degree above the brute, who will not love, better than before, the wife who sympathizes with and loves childhood? And this he may do—I believe he often does it—without reference to that increase of future domestic comfort and enjoyment of which it is eminently prophetic.

In short, I regard the love of childhood—simple, artless and pure as childhood in itself is—to be an important element of christian character. I have heard of—ay, I have known—persons who disliked children, some of whom were, in other respects, excellent men and women. But such a trait is certainly a great drawback upon human excellence. I will not say that they who hate infancy and childhood cannot be christians; but I may say that they cannot be, in this state of feeling, the perfect men and women they desire to be, nor the perfect children of their Father in heaven which they ought to be.

For do they not practically forget the affection—I was going to say the reverence—for the infantile nature, which was manifested by Him who said, "Of such is the kingdom of heaven?" Do they not forget, or at least overlook the fact, that our adorable Lord and Redeemer was a great lover of infancy, childhood and youth? And though they are sometimes tempted to turn aside, almost with a sneer, when they see adults and even old people caressing the young, would they turn away with disgust at the sight of our common Lord with little infants in his arms, and join with the crowd of his half followers and half disciples, to wonder at, if not to rebuke him?

Thus, whether we consider the health and longevity, the social, intellectual, moral and religious improvement, and the present and future happiness of the young wife, or the happiness of him whom she loves and esteems as she does herself, it is her unquestionable interest to strive with all her power, to love and respect infancy and childhood.

But is it possible, I shall be asked, to elicit, by cultivation, the love of childhood and the innocence of childhood, where it is wanting? Most undoubtedly. I have already shown that doing good produces love, in general; and I have incidentally mentioned some facts which bear directly on the point now before us. I have stated a case in which an adult, by cultivating the acquaintance of a child, soon became much attached to her society. Such, there can be but little doubt, would be the almost inevitable and unexceptionable result, in a majority of instances, where a similar course was attempted and persevered in. It is not in human nature, depraved as it is, to resist wholly the tendency of doing good to produce love in us for the person to whom it is done.

Let her, therefore, who is anxiously desirous of loving children, because she believes it would promote her own and the general happiness, commence a series of kind offices to those around her. Let her converse with them, answer their questions, tell them stories, hear theirs, and manifest an interest in their happiness. Let not this interest in their welfare be assumed—artificial—but sincere. Children will soon discover and detest the hypocrite. They love simplicity, they love sympathy, they return love for love; but they do not so readily return love for mere pretence—for hypocrisy.

Before all this, however—that is, in point of date—there must be faith. She who would bring herself to love childhood, must first believe it to be in her power to do so. She must also believe it to be her duty. Faith will remove mountains of difficulty. But without faith it is impossible—at least *almost* impossible—to do anything in the way of improvement. Both nature and revelation, for the most obvious reasons, put faith before works—the tree, in the order of precedence, before its fruits.

I wish this principle of putting faith before works was better understood. Blair, Addison, and other old fashioned moralists, tell us that we should fix on and pursue those habits which we know to be right and best for us, and custom will soon make them agreeable. Here faith, or the belief that the habit is best for us, is put in its proper place. In the same way, that is, on the same principle, as a general rule, may we bring ourselves to regard a fellow being, or the form of inanimate objects, or even the qualities of food, as agreeable. As soon as we believe it to be our duty to love childhood and infancy, that is, as soon as we have the faith which is the established pre-requisite, the work is more than begun; it is, prospectively speaking, half accomplished.

CHAPTER XXXI.

GIVING ADVICE.

Advice of females in regard to business. Why it is often undervalued. Objections answered. How far advice is applicable. Advice in manners and morals. Advice in religion.

If an individual has fallen into the society of one of those husbands—for such husbands there unfortunately are—who think it beneath their dignity to ask a wife's advice on any subject whatever, supposing her opinion to be of so little value as to be scarcely worth the trouble of obtaining, then it were better, perhaps, that she should omit this chapter, and only read those chapters which are more particularly adapted to her wants and circumstances.

But there are husbands to whom the advice of a wife will often be of great value; and it is for this reason, among many others, that a wife ought always to be interested in her husband's pursuits. Most sensible men expect this. They do not, indeed, expect them to understand, as intimately as themselves, all the details of their occupation; but only that they should have that general knowledge of it which will correspond to the knowledge which a farmer has of the common mechanical arts, or manufactures, or which the mechanic or manufacturer has of farming.

I have known some husbands who made it a point to tell their wives nothing at all about their own concerns, except occasionally, as a mere matter of favor!—or a tribute to their own praise. If they get a good bargain, which often means about the same thing as to defraud somebody, they are fond enough of relating the achievement. If they have had unusual success in some enterprise, and have just heard the welcome intelligence, they bring home the report. But as to keeping their wives constantly acquainted with the state of their affairs, they no more think of it than they do of communicating it to the Grand Seignior.

This treatment of the wife has very frequently one of these two effects :—It excites her curiosity, and leads her to be, at least at certain times, what he deems impertinently inquisitive, or it discourages and depresses her. In either case, the husband defeats his own intention.

Woman will not be treated as a slave or an ignoramus, with impunity. If she finds her husband has no confidence in her judgment, and gives her no account of his concerns, she ceases, at length, to take a deep interest in them, and indeed in everything which pertains to the happiness of matrimonial life. She will, indeed, continue to yield to him a sort of passive obedience, so far, at least, as not to displease him, nor subject herself to positive suffering; but as to making special exertions to promote his highest happiness, present and future, she will never do it. Indeed, why should it be expected? She falls more and more, especially from his example, into the way of acting from selfish motives; and what selfish purpose could she possibly gain by it? He seems happier in proportion as she possesses fewer rational attributes; and she accordingly not only ceases to make progress, but begins, ere long, to float down the stream of insignificance.

One reason which has been urged against making the wife familiarly acquainted with the husband's concerns of business is, that she will be likely to divulge things which it is for his interest to conceal. Woman, it is thought, finds it very difficult to keep a secret; and as there are many things in connection with a husband's business, which he may not wish to have the world know, it is considered safest to keep everything within his own bosom; and the less he says, even to his wife, the better.

Now that there are wives who cannot be safely entrusted with a secret, I have no doubt; yet I cannot help hoping they are few. Life cannot be spent very happily with a companion of whom we are every moment fearful, lest she should incautiously say something which she ought not. If a husband cannot trust his wife better than this, he has made a mistake, it would seem, in marrying her.

But it is said also that, after all, woman's advice is worth very little, even when she fully understands her husband's concerns, and is worthy of his entire confidence. Her judgment, it is said, was not intended by the Creator for such things, and is comparatively weak. To consult her about matters of business is to call her out of her own sphere.

That woman has her own appropriate sphere, and that this requires a cast of mind somewhat different, in its original structure, from that of man, there can be no doubt. Nor is it to be doubted that this circumstance, along with her habits, disqualifies her for *deciding* for the husband, in matters of business. But to advise is one thing, and to decide quite another.

It is woman's advice which a judicious husband wants, rather than her decisions. Her advice will be always valuable to him; but it will be more so, in proportion as she is endowed by nature and art with what is called good sense, and as she is made familiar with facts. The more, in these circumstances, he avails himself of her advice, the more valuable will he find it. And when I hear that such or such a wife has no judgment in regard to business matters, I usually think the fault is her husband's, in not having rendered her more familiar, day by day, with his business concerns, and trained her gradually to the habit of giving him her opinion.

The fact that a wife does not see the whole matter, as her husband does, will not disqualify her for advising. He must take the advice for just what it is worth, with her limited range of vision. If, from the nature of the case, he has reason to believe she sees but half the object, then he must make due allowance, and form corresponding expectations in regard to the results. To take the position that advice is of no value, unless the individual who gives it sees the whole case, is to maintain that nearly all the advice in the world is valueless.

He has certainly overlooked one important end of matrimony, who is not in the frequent practice of seeking this sort of assistance; that is, of ascertaining how, with the facts she has before her, a thing strikes his wife. Many an individual would have been saved from bankruptcy, had he done so; and from what are the frequent consequences of bankruptcy—intemperance, insignificance and crime.

But if it were granted that the advice of woman were less valuable, in this respect, than I have supposed—if her chief worth, as a counsellor to her husband, lay in her ability to afford him aid in manners and morals—her worth would still, in this respect alone, be inestimable.—I must remember, however, that I am not writing for husbands.

When the husband seeks the advice of his wife, let the subject be what it may, she should gladly embrace the opportunity of affording her assistance. Let her, however, be as careful that her opinion is well formed, as she is ready and willing to form and give it. She will thus lead him insensibly to regard her as his counsellor, and obtain an influence over him of which she had no previous conception.

For the more he seeks her advice, the more he will learn to regard it. It will, indeed, become, from day to day, and from year to year, more truly valuable, in its own nature. But this is not all. There is nothing, perhaps, in the whole compass of matrimonial life, that endears the parties more to each other, than the friendly offices to which I now refer. For it should not be overlooked, that what woman is ready to give, in this respect, she should also be ready to receive;—nay, she should be highly desirous of receiving it. On this point, further remarks are, I suppose, unnecessary; because woman, from her very nature and circumstances, is led almost involuntarily to man as a counsellor.

In short, here, as elsewhere, we come to the conclusion that matrimony is the natural state of man; that no individual of either sex is completely educated, or, in other words, rendered perfect, without it; and that the more we are accustomed to rely on each other as educators, the more we perceive each other's importance in the work of education; and the greater our usefulness and happiness here, and the more cheering our hopes of usefulness and happiness hereafter.

It is very frequently said that nothing is more difficult than for the husband and wife to converse together freely on their own religious state. Now if this is so, it is deeply unfortunate. Here it is, if anywhere on earth, that we ought to find the most intimate and free interchange of opinion and sentiment. If the wife cannot go to the husband with her difficulties, and seek his advice or instruction, to whom can she go? The minister is not always at hand; and if he were, would not always be the best adviser. She needs counsel and instruction, more than authority and dictation. And the same is true of the wants of the husband.

If the husband and wife regarded each other as religious counsellors, and sought each other's aid and assistance in their religious course from day to day—if their wants, difficulties, trials, doubts and fears were as frequently and as freely laid before each other as they are, or should be, before their great Friend and Counsellor on high, what a change would be effected in the condition of our race! How soon would this dark world be enlightened! How soon would it bloom as Eden! How soon would the wilderness and the solitary place be glad, and the moral desert begin to blossom as the rose!

It cannot be denied—it must be confessed—that instead of going first to these companions for life, for religious counsel, we often go to them, for this purpose, last. We seem to dread, in this respect, each other's society. A greater anomaly in human conduct can hardly exist; and yet it is a mistake which is almost universally made.

Let there be, in this particular, a thorough reform in social life. Let it be one prominent—perhaps I should say *the* prominent object of the husband and wife, to render each other all possible instruction and advice in the way to heaven. If the wife finds that a perpetual silence reigns on the subject, let her be the first to break it. Not indeed abruptly, but in an appropriate and discreet manner. She need not be an inquisitor, but only a friend.

Let her begin the work by her own example. She has some difficulty in regard to a passage of scripture. She seeks the husband's opinion in regard to its meaning. She has doubts in regard to the propriety of applying such a promise to her own case. She asks her husband to whom—to what general class of persons—he thinks it applicable. She gradually, in this way, unbosoms to him her own feelings and state, and gets his opinion and counsel. And in doing so repeatedly, he will be encouraged by her example to pursue the same course.

How strange it is, let me again say, that husbands and wives should, in these matters, stand at such a distance from each other.! How strange that three fourths of them should know less of each other's spiritual state, and hopes, and prospects, than they do of those of their neighbors! And why is it so? Is it not a great practical evil? Is it not an evil which is fundamental? And is it not one which demands immediate attention and correction?

As to times and seasons, I have little to say. If the husband's mind were not too frequently so crazed with business as to be totally unfitted for it, one of the most appropriate seasons for these mutual friendly offices would be the last hour before retiring to rest. Such a season has its advantages, in every point of view. But let there be some hour set apart for the purpose. If it be not made the work of a particular hour, or if, when the hour arrives for attending to it, we postpone it, or make it give place to other duties, no progress, we may be assured, will be made. If convinced that it is a work of the utmost importance to our present and eternal happiness, we must have our times and seasons for it; and these times and seasons must be as sacred to us as those of secret or family prayer, or the hours of the Sabbath.

CHAPTER XXXII.

SELF-GOVERNMENT.

Difficulties of self-government. Meaning of the term. Error in education. What is to be done? Motive to be presented. Directions how to proceed. Cooperation of the husband. The results happy.

NOTHING is more difficult than the work of self-government;—and for various reasons. One reason is, we are not trained to it. It is one of the last things which are secured, in modern education. I grant it is often talked about: but to talk about its importance is one thing—to attend to it, quite another.

Solomon observes—" He that hath no rule over his own spirit, is like a city that is broken down, and without walls;" and again—" He that ruleth his spirit is better than he that taketh a city." Socrates and Seneca, though without the light of christianity, or even of Judaism, appear not only to have understood this matter, but to have practised it, and to an extent which ought to put to the blush not a few who call themselves christians. " I would beat you," said Socrates, one day, to his servant, "if I were not angry." And Seneca says—"It is an idle thing to pretend that we cannot govern our anger;" and that "the wildest affections may be tamed by discipline."

It is not required of woman to preside in halls of justice, or to command armies; but it is required of her, no less than of the other sex, to do what is more difficult—to govern herself. It is required of every living, rational being, to rule or govern his own spirit. And the requisition is most reasonable and just.

I am not, however, speaking of governing ourselves in regard to temper alone. We are called to self-government in a thousand other ways, as well as in restraining our anger. All our affections, our passions and our appetites, are liable to exceed the bounds of moderation, unless they are duly regulated, and sometimes repressed. There is hardly an hour in a day of even the most placid life, in which we are not called to the work of self-government. It is true we do not always—perhaps, indeed, often—obey the call; and the reason is, as I have before said, that we are not accustomed to it. We are not inured to the yoke from our youth.

Not only do some parents, and teachers, and educators, neglect to train us, by example and precept, to govern ourselves, but they go farther, and lead us into temptation. We are surrounded, from our earliest infancy, with almost every form of physical and mental excitement; and then, left as we are without the habit of self-denial, what wonder is it, if we make shipwreck?

We will suppose, however, that we have so far escaped as to reach in safety the harbor of matrimony. Suppose, still farther, that we see with clearness the perils and dangers to which we have been exposed. We see, too, that there are dangers still before us; that without self-government—without daily effort and self-denial—the voyage of life is still perilous, to ourselves and others. What is to be done?

Shall we give up the point—perhaps at the early age of twenty—and conclude that our case is hopeless?—that our education is complete—all our habits formed, and our character, for time and for eternity, fixed beyond the hope of alteration? By no means. To do so would be to act in a manner wholly unworthy of the dignity of our nature, as well as wholly contrary to the will of Him who bestowed it.

It is indeed true that, as a fact of every-day life, human character is generally formed, and human destiny determined, long before we reach the age of twenty years. But it need not be so. Man is susceptible of reformation, in a remarkable degree, long after this period. The reason why so few are reformed, in point of fact, at this late period, is not so much because they are unsusceptible of change, as because they have not a hearty desire to be changed. Present to the individual a motive strong enough, and the difficulties in the way will soon gradually disappear. A few of the most useful of our race were, in early life, wholly unpromising. This is an encouragement, not to delay, but against despair. What man has done, man may do.

Such a motive I would gladly present to the young wife. She finds herself, I am to suppose, at the age of twenty, united for life to one whom she earnestly loves, and desires to make happy. She has been taught the road to happiness, both for herself and her husband. She knows, in some degree, the strength of her passions and propensities. She knows when and where she ought to resist them. But to practical resistance she has never been accustomed; and therefore when she would do good, evil is present with her. The temptation comes; but habit has rendered her will weak and yielding, and she is carried away by the force of the current. She laments over it—reproaches herself for it—promises amendment. But the temptation again recurs, her will is still weak, and she is again overcome by it.

And thus she goes on. She knows the right, and would pursue it; she knows the wrong, and yet follows it. This she could better endure, if it affected no one but herself. But her husband, too, is a sufferer from her example, and perhaps others. She would break the spell that binds her, but how can she? How shall she take the first step?

She must remove, as much as possible, every temptation. She knows that exciting food—food, I mean, which is high-seasoned, or indigestible—affects her unhappily. Let her then exchange it for that which is better. She knows that late evening hours, especially if she have company, affect her nervous system: let her learn to retire early. She believes fully in the evil tendency of coffee and tea: let her, then, banish them from her table. She knows, in one word, that every physical error affects her moral and intellectual character, more or less, and renders her, in a greater or less degree, unable to deny herself that which she knows to be wrong, and even indirectly weakens her power to restrain her propensities, and govern her temper. She knows, moreover, that every act of disobedience to conscience, even in the smallest matter, has a tendency which is plainly and directly efficacious, in weakening her already feeble will, and inducing her to fall under the power of temptation.

She must therefore resolve strongly to do right in the smallest matters. It is in vain, or almost in vain, for people to do wrong daily and hourly—perhaps a dozen times an hour—in the smaller concerns of life, and yet expect to govern themselves in larger matters. And yet three fourths of mankind seem not so to understand it. They suffer themselves to do wrong with impunity—even to the extent of harboring feelings of anger or revenge, in the little things of life, and yet wonder they cannot keep their good resolutions of amendment in the greater trials. No mistake can be greater, or more fatal.

Let the wife understand this, precisely as it is, and let her form her resolution and begin her work accordingly. Let it not be delayed. To put it off to-day, is almost equivalent to a guaranty that it shall be put off to-morrow. Let her begin now, and let her begin strongly.

There is one circumstance, perhaps, which might justify delay—at least, the delay of a moment. It is the prospect of bringing your husband to a conclusion to join you. The hope of starting at the same time, in such a glorious work, and of journeying on together, is certainly a just cause for delay—at least, for a few days. Besides, it is not wholly lost time. You have a longer season for reflection on the nature of your undertaking, of strengthening your resolution to persevere, and of seeking counsel from above.

There is nothing more delightful than to see a young wife taking the lead in a work of this kind, and persevering. We have seen already that self-government is no light affair. We have seen—at least, I hope it has been made plain—that on it depends, under God, much of the comfort and happiness of matrimonial life.

The sight is delightful, not only for its immediate, but for its prospective advantages. To be the means of conquering one's self, and of leading a husband to a similar victory, is high praise. But this is not all, nor indeed the most. It is but the prelude of a better day to coming generations. In proportion as parents can be induced to undertake the work of self-education, and to acquire the habit of completely governing themselves in all the relations, and circumstances, and conditions of life, in just the same proportion may we look forward with confidence to a reform, in this respect, in our whole system of modern education, both in the family and in the schools. It is next to impossible for parents to taste the joys and blessings of such a conquest, and not be desirous of preventing, in their children, that which it has cost them so much pains to remove or correct.

If the work which has thus been proposed were beyond the capability of the young wife, or if it were within the reach or ability of a favored few only, I would insist upon it less strongly. But I regard it, on the contrary, as quite within the reach and means of all. And happy are they who, finding out the errors of their early education, begin and persevere in the work of educating and reforming themselves, before it is too late. It is, indeed, never too late, wholly so, while life lasts; but the earlier we begin, the better. We shall do comparatively little, if we do not commence before we are forty.

But happy is the woman who, by a favorable education, has been thoroughly established in good habits from the very first—whose meat and whose drink it is to take up her cross and govern herself daily. She enters upon the matrimonial state prepared to go forward at once with joy and hope, having escaped both the hindrance and the misery of a late repentance.

CHAPTER XXXIII.

INTELLECTUAL IMPROVEMENT.

Anecdote of Mrs. H. Course of study after marriage. Much of it excellent. Cooperation of the husband and wife. Nature of education. Difficulties of studying in married life. They may be overcome. Importance of system. Evils of a want of it. Anecdote. Chemistry. Its importance illustrated by anecdotes and facts. Terrible consequences of ignorance in housewifery. Much poisoning in the community. Study of other sciences. Anatomy and physiology. A few books recommended. Collateral topics of study. Knowledge necessary to benevolent effort. Study of the subject of education. Errors. Theory and experience.

Mrs. H. was early married to a person much older and better instructed than herself—a lawyer by profession. He was one of those men, however, who place intellectual and moral improvement higher than all things earthly; and who will not forego the improvement of themselves and their own families, for the sake of distant and more uncertain advantages, however large in the prospect. Mrs. H., in short, became, in effect, her husband's pupil. The following is her own account of the progress she made while under the instruction of her new teacher.

"Under his instruction and example, my prose style of writing, which the critics generally allow to be 'pure idiomatic English,' was formed. I acknowledge that my early predilection was for the pompous words and sounding periods of Johnson, and I had greatly admired the sublime flights and glittering fancies of Counsellor Phillips, the Irish orator, then in the meridian of his fame; but my husband convinced me, by analyzing his sentences, that they were, as he had called them, 'sublime nonsense.'

"We commenced, immediately after our marriage, a system of study, which we pursued together, with few interruptions, and these unavoidable, during his life. The hours we allotted were from eight o'clock in the evening till ten. In this manner we studied French and botany, (then almost a new science in this country, but for which my husband had an uncommon taste,) and obtained some knowledge of mineralogy, geology, &c., besides pursuing a long and instructive course of reading."

I had not intended to quote farther from this instructive autobiographical sketch of a young wife; but some of my readers may be interested to know the results; and they are so truly instructive, that I venture to proceed.

"In all our mental pursuits, it seemed the aim of Mr. H. to enlighten my reason, strengthen my judgment, and give me confidence in my own powers of mind, which he estimated much higher than I did. I equalled him in imagination, but in no other faculty. Yet the approbation which he bestowed on my talents has been a great encouragement to me, in attempting the duties which were to be my portion.

"In short, had we known the future, the course pursued could not have been more judicious. But such a result seemed utterly improbable; for he enjoyed the most perfect health, while mine was very delicate. Still I was to be the survivor;—he died suddenly, as with a stroke—and with him seemed to expire every earthly hope. His business was large, for the country, but he had hardly reached that age when men of his profession begin to lay up property, and he had spared no indulgence to his family. We had lived in comfort; but I was left poor.

"For myself, the change added not one particle to my grief; but for my children, I was deeply distressed. I had five—the eldest only seven years of age: how were these to be supported and educated? I cared not that they should inherit wealth—I never coveted great riches—but to be deprived of the means of education, was to make them 'poor indeed.' At length, after revolving the subject deeply in my mind, I attempted to provide for their education myself, in some measure as their father would have done. I resolved to devote my whole earthly care to that one object, and, relying on Providence, to go onward, whatever obstacles might impede.

"I am sure that the benevolent reader will be glad to learn that I have been, thus far, successful in my design. My eldest son, educated at West Point, is now a lieutenant in the United States' service, and from his small pay assists me; and my other children are so far advanced in that course of education I had marked out, as to give me good reason to believe that I shall, in a few years, see them intelligent and useful members of the community."

It is, of course, no purpose of mine to express an opinion, in this place, in favor of the entire "course" of Mrs. H., for herself and family. My object is, rather, to show what has been done, and consequently, what others can do; and, at all events, to encourage study, and a plan of some sort.

I should never select, as a season of study, the time between eight and ten o'clock in the evening;

but perhaps Mrs. H. had it not in her power to select her season. Perhaps her husband's engagements were of such a nature as to leave him no other season or opportunity. It is difficult to believe this, however. It is difficult to conceive of any circumstances which should prevent the possibility of sleeping from eight to ten, and rising and studying from four to six in the morning, which would have been far more favorable, both to body and mind.

But after every necessary abatement, the case is one of great importance and interest. Mrs. H. was not deficient in talent, natural or acquired, when she was married. Yet a plan was immediately laid for carrying on, through life, an education which had been auspiciously begun. It was not only laid, but put in immediate execution. And above all—which is the highest praise—it was persevered in. Too many plans of this kind, happily begun, prove abortive, for want of the spirit of perseverance.

The object of this education was also elevated and important. It was not so much to fill her head with the facts of botany, mineralogy or geology, as to cultivate reason, judgment and faith. It was to fit her, in one word, for the great work of female life. It was to educate her in such a manner as would best prepare her to educate others.

And these, for a time, she did educate. It was no small task to have the care of five children, the eldest of whom was but seven years old—in poverty, too; and what is still worse, with feeble health. No wonder, perhaps, that a mother thus situated, and probably without servants, should feel depressed; and however prepared by Providence to sustain the burden and the task, after a struggle for years, should yield to the temptation which is presented by our fashionable male and female boarding schools, and send her children from home, though at increased expense, as well as risk of character, to complete their education.

I do not here undertake to say that a young wife should wait for the cooperation of her husband. But it is a very happy circumstance, if she finds him ready to cooperate with her, even at the expense of a little solicitation. It is more, indeed, than can often be expected. Few there are who will find a husband ready to go forward in such a work; and therefore few ought to expect it. I grant that the benefits are in a degree mutual. No husband can pursue a course of study in any science, with his wife, even though he were tolerably familiar with it before, without deriving signal benefit from it. And if this were the place, I would press upon the husband the exceeding great importance of such a cooperation. I would conjure him to attend to a system of intellectual improvement, for his own sake; but much more for the sake of her whom he holds most dear, and for the sake of those over whom she is destined to have a strong and lasting influence.

The education of the school is only a preparation for a future and more extended course of study. I know it is often considered otherwise. I know it is often thought—at least, if we may judge of people's thoughts by their practice—that our education is completed when we leave the school. Or if there are a few who think otherwise—if here and there an individual is found who will continue his studies afterward, it is only till marriage. Matrimony puts an end, usually, to study—I mean, to the study of scientific subjects. Perhaps not one married individual in a thousand—I fear the proportion is much smaller still—ever thinks or dreams of making any farther progress, after the wedding day is over.

And why not? Can a single reason be given in favor of study the week before marriage, which shall not be equally in favor of studying the week afterwards? Is knowledge less necessary? Is it less pleasant or desirable? Are our duties or our obligations diminished? Strange, if it were so. Strange that as our relations—the points at which we touch the world we live in—are multiplied, our duties should be diminished, and the lights of science and the treasures of human wisdom become less highly prized, or less necessary.

It is said that the new relations and new duties which marriage imposes consume our time, and we have fewer opportunities for making progress than before. Yes, they do, if we must follow all the fashions—if we must make as many unmeaning calls, and receive as much trifling or useless company, as the customs of high life, in modern times, demand, and if our system of house-keeping must conform to an arbitrary standard—one which, instead of being based on the love of God and man, has for its support—its very pillars—the whim and caprice of fools.

But is there any necessity for this? Are we not bound, on the contrary, as christians, to set our faces, by our practice, against such customs? Are we not bound, in the fear of God, to make such arrangements in regard to our houses, our help, our furniture, our everything, as will give time for all necessary improvement of the mind? Is it not an obvious wrong—a serious one—to pursue a course, as multitudes do, which shall effectually exclude it?

When I allude to unmeaning calls and useless company, I am far from intending to intimate that all our calls—all social intercourse—should be banished. On the contrary, I consider social intercourse as indispensable as our daily bodily food; and on this point, I shall say something in a future chapter. But I do say, with the utmost confidence, that a kind of social intercourse which excludes individual study—which, in short, prevents married life from being a school for mutual improvement, even in science—is not to be encouraged by those who call themselves christians, nor even by those who lay claim to an ordinary share of sound common sense.

I care not how wise the young wife or the young husband may be, when their union is consummated. I care not if they are both as wise as the distinguished female with whose history I commenced this chapter. I care not, did I say? It is not so. I do care. The wiser the better. The wiser they are, the more true wisdom they possess—the greater will be the security that the fires which are applied to the altar of Hymen will not, at the same time, destroy all books and study. Mrs. H. came not to the altar with an uncultivated mind. It was her love of study, joined to that of her husband, which led them to plan and execute a project, the effects of which will be felt in future generations, until time shall be no longer. Nor did the whole care and burden of five very young children smother the thirst for knowledge which a long course of mutual study had enkindled.

It is far from being in my power to point out a course of study which shall be adapted to the wants and circumstances of all young married people. The previous studies and modes of thinking, and especially the predilections, will and should be considered, especially if the young wife is to study alone. If she is to have the company of her husband, his habits and preferences too, are to be taken into consideration ; and one or the other must make concessions—not to say sacrifices : I mean, of inclination. The wife, perhaps, will be fond of natural science, while the husband will be fond of history—civil, political and ecclesiastical. Or she will prefer botany, while he prefers chemistry. But there is no need of difficulty. Each, for the sake of the other, must be willing to yield their own preferences ; and no wife of good sense will prefer studying botany alone, as the first step, to the pursuit of a highly valuable science in which she can have company. She should be especially ready to yield her will to his, in matters of this kind, when she considers that it is less the object of all education to teach facts—to impart knowledge, properly so called—than to discipline the mental powers and faculties.

And yet, free to make this confession as I am, I am still of opinion that improvement in mere science is of inestimable importance to all mankind; and to no person more so than the young housewife. Her great business, as I have repeatedly said, is education. She takes not a step which does not educate herself, her husband or others. So surely as she lifts a finger, or utters a word, or gives a direction, or casts an approving or disapproving look, that modifies the feelings, or the affections, or the conduct, or the health, of those around her, so surely does she become their educator—the former of their character for time or for eternity, or both. I know I am liable to repeat, in forms scarcely varied, this truth. But I am not unwilling to do so. It is a great and important truth; and were it as well applied by christians as it is understood and admitted by them in theory, it would materially change the aspect of the whole civilized world.

To those who are duly prepared for the work, nothing will afford more intense interest than the study of education. The great difficulty to be met, in this pursuit, is the want of suitable books.

One who is determined on mastering this great science may, indeed, derive much light from books of various kinds, in different departments. The Bible is full of instruction to the young educator, embodied not only in abstract principles, but in living examples. So is profane history. So is biography. So is narrative, and even fiction. In short, go where we will, in books or among men, and the volume of education is wide open, in which "he who runs may read."

There are books, however, which are particularly adapted to the wants of the young educator. Nor are they so rare as might at first view be supposed. It is not true, though the statement has often been made, that we have no books on education. A long catalogue might be made out, if this were the place for it, of just such volumes as would be eagerly read by any individual whose mind has been so far expanded as to perceive, in this respect, its own ignorance, and who has acquired either a thirst for knowledge in this department, or a desire for improvement in general.

But pursue what subject she may, alone or in company, the young wife must be systematic. She must have her hours for study, and those must be sacred to that object. No ordinary circumstance must be an excuse for omitting it a single day. It is true that there are difficulties in the way of carrying out a plan of this kind. The last hours of the day or the first in the morning are undoubtedly the best; and as I have elsewhere said, I greatly prefer the latter. I do so because the head is then usually most clear, and the body and mind most vigorous; because it is a season for study more favorable to health than the evening, and because it is a season in which there is less probability of interruption than in any other.

I insist upon a set time for study, especially for married people, because I do not believe a successful course, on the most favorite topic or science, will ever be pursued under any other circumstances. Life is made up of so much variety, and there are so many demands, in one form or another, upon our time, that if we do not fix upon a particular season, and adhere to it, we shall gradually be led, almost inevitably, to omit it altogether.

I knew a young couple who set out in life with the most determined resolution to make it a part of their daily duty to study some favorite science. But they had never agreed upon a particular hour, or branch of study; and for the first few weeks after their union, found it somewhat difficult to fix upon any subject or season which was not objectionable. One preferred history; the other geology. One preferred the evening; the other the morning. One was disposed to delay the work for a few months, until such an object was accomplished, and such an arrangement completed; the other chose to go on immediately. At length a book of great general interest coming in their way,

INTELLECTUAL IMPROVEMENT.

it was decided to read that together at stated intervals, and take up the study of something, *as a study*, at a future time. But as no hour was fixed upon, this was not done. Not a quarter of the book was read until another appeared of greater interest, and the first was abandoned. Perhaps the second was read through, though I am not certain even of this.

But of one thing I am certain, which is, that though a few books were read, a greater number were begun and never finished; and the study of any particular science was deferred from month to month, till the lapse of almost a year, when mutual shame for their delay drove them to resolve on something, and upon a set time in which to do it; and now it was, and not until now, that a course of study was commenced in earnest, which, it may be hoped, will not be discontinued except with the life of one of the parties.—I say, therefore, that the great point is to fix on a subject, and make a beginning, and pursue that subject uninterruptedly till it is finished; I mean, till we have gone as far in it as we intended on setting out. The pleasure of mastering a work is, to most persons, the highest reward for their past toil, and the most powerful stimulus to future exertion.

If I were to mention a single science which I conceive to be of importance to house-keepers, it would be chemistry. I speak now, however, of the sciences which have usually been taught in our schools and colleges. For, independent of custom or public sentiment, I regard human anatomy and physiology as the science which stands first in point of importance to all mankind; but as second to this, and perhaps introductory to it, on the list, I place chemistry.

The importance of chemistry to the housewife, though admitted in words, seems, after all, but little understood. How can we hope to urge her forward to the work of ventilating and properly cleansing her apartments and her furniture, until she understands not only the native constitution of our atmosphere, but the nature of the changes which this atmosphere undergoes in our fire rooms, our sleeping rooms, our beds, our cellars, and our lungs? How can we expect her to cooperate, with all her heart, in the work of simplifying and improving cookery, simplifying our meals, and removing, step by step, from our tables, objectionable articles, or deleterious compounds, until she understands effectually the nature and results of fermentation, as well as of mastication and digestion? How can we expect her to detect noxious gases, and prevent unfavorable chemical changes, and the poisonous compounds which sometimes result, and which have again and again destroyed health and life, while she is as ignorant as thousands are, who are called housewives, of the first principles of chemical science? Would it not be to expect impossibilities?

A great multitude of facts might be stated to illustrate the importance of a knowledge of the principles of chemistry to those who have the superintendence of household concerns, from which, however, I will select only one or two of the more prominent.

Late in the autumn of 1814, a severe disease broke out at Elizabethtown, in Pennsylvania, and many who were attacked with it died. It was subsequently traced by the physicians, among whom was the distinguished Dr. Eberle, to the following cause:—The manufacture of common red earthen ware had been recently commenced in that neighborhood, and many of the inhabitants, for the first time, had supplied themselves with the wares; and among the rest, with a quantity of deep jars. Into these jars they had put their apple butter, or apple sauce. The acid of the apple sauce coming in contact with the glazing, which consisted of an oxyd of lead, had dissolved it, and formed acetate of lead (sugar of lead.)

The effects of sugar of lead, when received into the human stomach, are pretty well known. It is a slow but sure poison; and when taken in any considerable quantity, or in a smaller quantity for a long time, gives rise to what is called painters' colic. The people of Elizabethtown had eaten very freely of the apple sauce; and the sugar of lead which it contained produced the terrible results.

Now I have no doubt that multitudes of individuals in our community are poisoned more or less in the same way. A great many—probably a majority of the families of this community—use this very sort of ware more or less every year; and not a few of them put acids into it. I have seen numbers of these jars in daily family use, with the glazing off; and have no reason to doubt that somebody had been poisoned with it. I do not say that they were probably destroyed; for nothing is more common, than for culinary poisons to produce mischief, whose effects do not become visible for months or years.

On this subject I must be permitted to linger for a moment. People tell us, in reply to remarks like the foregoing—" Why, we have always used these jars in our family, more or less, and our fathers before us, and nobody has ever been poisoned;" or in reply to our remarks about the danger of eating or drinking certain mixtures or compounds—" Why, it has always been customary to use them, and yet, forsooth, you have just now found out they are injurious." Yes, it has always been customary to use them, I grant; but it has also been customary to be sick. How do you know how much of the disease which has prevailed in the community has been the effect of the very causes of which I am speaking?

Diseases are chiefly produced by the errors of mankind, in one way or another; and is it not reasonable to believe that a very full proportion of them are the result of the ignorance or unskilfulness of housewives? He who is most ready to answer this question negatively, is probably least acquainted with facts.

How many times have I seen apples which were baked or stewed in an iron bason, turned brown or almost black by the process. They are stained by the kettle, we are told. And yet the kettle is clean. The truth is, the acid of the apple combines with a small portion of oxydized iron, and forms a substance not unlike copperas, which colors the apples. If the acid which is thus active is, in reality, the sulphuric acid—I suppose it is not—the substance which is formed is sulphate of iron, or copperas—a compound which everybody knows is rank poison. At any rate, there is every reason to fear that most kinds of food which are colored, as it is called, by the kettle or vessel in which they are prepared or kept, is poisoned.

But these are only specimens of the mischief to which the community are exposed by the ignorance of housewives upon this subject. I might mention hundreds of others. I might prove that the hand of ignorance cannot set a fashionable table in a single instance, without endangering, in a greater or less degree, the health of those who are to partake of the immense variety of its contents, either by presenting something which is poisonous before it is received, or which becomes poisonous by new chemical combinations.

I know it is doubted by many whether chemical changes ever take place in a healthy stomach; and such persons will at once say that what is not poisonous before it is taken into the stomach, cannot become poisonous after it is received. Granted this were true, it would not follow that these changes could not take place in a stomach which is diseased, or even debilitated; and as I am ready to maintain that nearly every human stomach is thus at fault, more or less, the results to the individual may still be as I have supposed.

In fact, a person may be poisoned, in a certain sense, by suddenly returning from a luxurious to a simple course of eating. Suppose he had been long in the habit of using much animal food, which is highly alkaline and exciting. He suddenly abandons it, but not only continues the same quantity of food as before which has an acid tendency, and whose over-acidity the meat had hitherto operated to correct, but, by way of compensation for his abstinence from flesh, greatly increases its quantity. The stomach, too, in the case supposed, having been long excited by the presence of the flesh meat, appears for a time to be debilitated. How long, in these circumstances, will it be before there will be a predominance of acid in this organ? And how long, if the evil is continued, before the individual will become the prey of disease?

Is it then unsafe to return from bad to correct habits? By no means, if the return is gradual. No, nor if the return is sudden, provided it is done according to science. But the danger is in making sudden changes at hap-hazard.

I have dwelt at so much length on the danger of ignorance in a housewife, that I must reluctantly omit many other illustrations of equal, perhaps superior importance. I might attempt to show how many thousands of the human race, in a highly civilized, or rather an over-refined state, have become the victims of scrofula, consumption, bowel complaints, dropsy in the head, &c. &c. through the mother's ignorance of the laws of chemistry and physiology.

The notion that this view would impeach the wisdom and goodness of the Creator, is not true. The Creator did not, philosophically speaking, create the present state of things. What we call a state of high cultivation and refinement, is no more the workmanship of the Creator than a mere savage state; nor does it much better promote his purposes in the redemption of man. Without the balance wheel of pure and undefiled christianity, society will probably continue to vibrate from the extreme of a savage state on the one hand, to the extreme of a sensual refinement on the other, and from the latter to the former. Our hope is, that with it, whenever its influences shall be made to pervade the whole social—especially the domestic —circle, it will probably settle down into a happy medium between the two.

Natural philosophy is also of great value, as a science, to the house-keeper. So is botany; and so is zoology, and indeed almost every branch of natural history. But of all the natural sciences, anatomy and physiology, together with the natural history of man, are preeminently important to the mistress of every family, whether her influence is to be greater or smaller. For this, chemistry— domestic chemistry, at least—is one of the best possible preparatives; and it is for this reason, in part, that so much space has been devoted to the consideration of its importance.

Anatomy and physiology, together with the natural history of man, may be a leading subject of study for years. I can conceive of no topic, except religion, which will be at once so valuable as a discipline to the mental faculties, so rich in instruction, as a means of future usefulness, or so full of interest in the pursuit; provided, however, a few obstacles can be overcome, which usually present themselves at our entrance upon the course. I allude to the unnatural association in most minds of anatomy and physiology with the mangling of living bodies, and to the difficulty of obtaining suitable books to assist us.

The first difficulty can only be overcome gradually, as we proceed in our course. The second is not to be overcome wholly, till some of those who are capable of performing the task, have prepared for us a set of better books for popular use than any which have hitherto appeared on the subject. Something, however, may be accomplished with the few books we have—imperfect as most of them are, and full of technicalities. As to removing all difficulties in the pursuit of science, it is scarcely to be expected; nor is it desirable. It is the effort to overcome difficulties that, more than anything else, gives strength to human character.

If I were to recommend to a young couple what course to take in the study of anatomy and physiology, I would say—Begin with Paley's Theology. Then take up and read Combe's Constitution of Man, rejecting, if you choose, the phrenological part; though if a person has time enough I would advise him to study phrenology. Next to Combe's work, I should recommend the study of Lawrence's Lectures on Physiology, Zoology, and the Natural History of Man. Combe's Principles of Physiology may now be advantageously studied; and afterward some of the more complete and scientific works on physiology. By this time, and not in my opinion before, if the circumstances will possibly admit of so much delay, we are prepared to study books on health, such as Johnson's Economy of Health, Willich's Lectures on Diet and Regimen, Dunglison's Elements of Hygiene, &c.

Nor is it much sooner that the young wife can, with entire safety, study the nature or cure of disease, either infantile or adult. Indeed, as I have elsewhere shown, I do not think the study of medicine and disease, properly so called, to be a part of human duty, except as a matter of curiosity, and with a view to prevention. If parents knew the nature of disease, and especially its causes, it would undoubtedly aid them greatly in the work of prevention; and with this view—and not to render every one " his own doctor "— I am willing they should look over such a work as Buchan's Domestic Medicine.

I have taken it for granted, that in the study of this great subject, the husband and the wife proceed together. If not—if the wife were to proceed alone, and without so much as the sympathy of her husband, the course I should recommend would be somewhat different; though perhaps not essentially so. The principal point of variation would consist in the alternation of physiological with collateral subjects; as travels, voyages, geography, history, and especially the Bible. All these, while they acquaint us with human nature, externally and internally, do, at the same time, afford us much information in regard to man's physiological and dietetic character.

Those who have never paid an hour's attention, in their whole lives, to the science of human life, have no conception of the immense advantages it would give them, not only in forming a proper estimate of character, in general, but in directing their efforts in every measure which concerns human improvement. The minister of the gospel will labor to far greater purpose—other things being equal—when he understands the whole nature of those for whose benefit he labors. The christian parent—the father or the mother—will perform his task, I had almost said infinitely better, when he understands the physical nature of those whom God has directed him to train up in the way they should go. The same may be said of all sorts of teachers. And I might add, in conclusion, that the same might be said of every individual under the whole heaven, who has received but the second table of the moral law—Thou shalt love thy neighbor as thyself. Constituted as the world now is, and involved, as it is, in a general moral obliquity from Jehovah, which a pseudo refinement has by no means a tendency to remove, it is, to say the least, questionable whether an individual effort can be made for its renovation in any respect, which would not be at least two fold more effective when made under the light and guidance of physiological knowledge.

The call is often made, in these times, on the young wife, to embark in a war against vice in some of its more heinous or offensive forms ; and the individual has, of course, no alternative but to enlist or refuse. But if she refuses, she is expected to be able to give her reasons. Can she do this ? What female sufficiently understands thoroughly these subjects ?

Let me not be understood, in this place, as calling in question the propriety of voluntary associations for the accomplishment of benevolent purposes. Whatever my private opinion may be on this point, this is not the place for it. What I principally insist on is, that since woman, in the present attitude of society, is continually called upon to act or refrain from acting, it is of very great importance that she should act right.

Suppose, for example, she is expected to join what is now called a "Moral Reform Society." She has no doubt of the existence of the evils which it is the object of these associations to remove. Or if she had doubts on the subject, a judicious lecturer would probably, in a single hour, remove them. But the question is—how shall they be removed? In order to understand this, it is necessary to trace them to their causes. But this I venture to say, without the light of physiology, she cannot do. Yet, without knowing the causes either of moral or physical evil, we labor in the dark to remove it. We may strike right, or we may not; all is a matter of hap-hazard.

So it is in regard to intemperance. Females are expected to associate for the removal of this desolating scourge. But will they move a step for this purpose in the dark? Will they join in an attack on an evil of whose causes—yes, and whose nature, too—they are grossly ignorant? Yes, they can; as facts will abundantly testify. They can, if they will, proceed in ignorance, as many of the other sex do. They can join in efforts to remove a thing which they do not understand. But to remove one branch of a noxious shrub or tree is not to destroy it. The wiser course would be to undermine, or dig up and destroy, the parent stock.

It is certainly proper and seemly for females who engage in the benevolent projects of the present day, to know how to apply their efforts. If the foundations of intemperance and licentiousness are laid in the family, before the infant has emerged from the cradle—if the seeds of these terrible woes are sown by mothers and nurses, and those who inhabit the abodes of infancy, and guide and direct the infantile affections—if the hot tea, and the strong coffee, and the cider barrel, and the high seasoned food, first tempt the drunkard into the broad but downward road, and the amorous looks, and tones, and language of those who even think themselves pure " in all manner of conversation," first pave the way to licentiousness—is it not almost in vain for the mother to leave the domestic circle to join in a crusade, be it ever so holy or so necessary, against evils which have their origin under her own eye, or at least within her own precincts ? Will she not do more by being, as the apostle terms it, a keeper at home ? Or if not—

if she is mistaken in her views—is it no source of satisfaction to her to be able to state her objections when she refuses to join in noisy public measures?

But this, I say again, no female can understandingly do, until she has become a thorough student in physiology. She will then learn—and not before—that if "temperance in all things" is her motto, she is already constituted by the Creator the president of a Society within her own doors; and that she is not likely soon to be out of a sphere for benevolent effort.

These views lead us once more to the remark, that the great office of women is that of an educator. And if so, it may now be added, that her favorite-topic of study should be education. Not mere instruction; for that is but a part—I think a very small part—of education; but the formation of character, physical, intellectual, social, moral and religious—its formation, both for time and for eternity.

Many persons turn away in disgust at the idea of studying education as a science. They seem to suppose that skill to train up the young is accidental; or rather that it is a peculiar gift of Heaven bestowed upon a few; and that the mass of parents and teachers, study it as much as they may, must forever grope their way in the world without it.

It would be strange indeed, if the command to train up a child in the way he should go, were given to all mankind, while only a few were able to follow it. Yet such, if we examine the case, is the general belief. They admit that we are commanded to train up children for God; and yet they think the greater part of our race so constituted by nature that the thing cannot be done. First, that constitutional defects are in the way. One child, we are told, is naturally of such an unmanageable temper, or has such a natural temperament, that he cannot be governed. Secondly, we are told that many of us are born without the talent or faculty, as I have heard it called, of governing.

Now no reasonable person will deny that there are constitutional differences both in children and adults. Nor will any one, as it seems to me, deny that some persons have not the art or capacity to govern. They were never themselves taught to obey; and herein is the grand difficulty.

What is first wanted in a person, is faith in himself; confidence in his own capacity for improvement. When this is acquired, and a course of study settled on, the work of self-education and of fitting ourselves to train others, for God and for eternity, is already, in prospect, achieved. "He hath his work half done, who hath it well begun," is an old maxim; but he hath it more than half done who hath begun it with faith. There is a deep and important meaning in the statement, that faith can remove mountains.

The young wife who has begun a course of chemical or physiological study with full faith in her power to understand it and render her knowledge available, will find encouragement at every step of her progress. Then when she comes to study history, sacred and profane, she will find her knowledge of herself and those around her deepened from almost every page. She learns from it what are the great springs of human action. This is especially true of the study of sacred history. So ample is the knowledge of humanity as well as of divinity, which the study of the Bible imparts, that I have sometimes thought, for the moment, we needed no other volume on education than this. But when I come to reflect farther, I do not fail to perceive that other volumes have their advantages.

When a broad view has been taken of the fields of natural science, and the Bible has been extensively, and warmly, and *faithfully* studied as a key to the mind and heart, it will be useful to examine some of the better systems of mental philosophy. The philosophy of the mind can never be too well understood; and he who thinks his knowledge of human nature is already profound enough, and on this account refuses to read books which treat on the subject, affords the best possible evidence of his own ignorance.

It will be seen that I have advanced, in the last paragraphs, very different views from those usually entertained on two points, viz., the acquisition of a knowledge of human nature, and of the art of governing and educating. The general opinion has been, that the former is only acquired from observation and experience, and that books furnish us no aid, and that the latter is a peculiar gift, with which reading and the study of books have little or nothing to do. Whereas, I maintain that the study of man, in books on chemistry, physiology, history and philosophy, though not sufficient of itself to do everything, is yet an indispensable aid; and when common sense is not wanting, may effect great changes in the whole character of the individual who studies them.

Nothing will be sooner repelled by most people than the charge that they are ignorant of human nature. You may represent them as ignorant of almost everything else but this, and they will endure it. But in the knowledge of human nature every one is ready to regard himself as not merely skilful, but profound. And yet, if the view I have taken of the general state of things is correct, this is among the best of proofs of our ignorance of the very subject on which we most pride ourselves.

There is however a dislike, almost equally general, to studying the subject of education. Many who think it important to read and investigate on nearly every other topic refuse to read or think on this. They will often purchase books and subscribe for periodicals to the extent of a hundred dollars a year, embracing almost every topic of the day ; but present to them the claims of a work on education of the highest celebrity and most acknowledged importance, and they are prone to turn away with indifference, if not with disgust.

This is a work on education, and will therefore, it may be, share the same fate. It certainly will, unless the reader brings to the task of its perusal very different views and feelings from many which at the present day prevail. It will, if she comes to its perusal with the vague, but general belief that she is too old to improve by reading or study on any subject, whether of much or little importance. It will, if she cannot get rid of the prevalent notion that the art of governing and educating the young is one of mere hap-hazard ; one on which books—I had almost said reason—have little to do. It will, also, if she cannot get rid of the erroneous idea, that she has no time to devote to the important business of educating herself, or preparing to aid in the education of others.

I am not ignorant of the grand objection, brought at the present day, to all efforts for self-improvement—a want of time. We hear it from everybody, at all ages above the merest childhood—and from persons of all circumstances and conditions. If there be a difference, however, we hear it most frequently from those who are in the best circumstances, in a pecuniary point of view; and who ought to be the least forward to make it.

But let me say, once for all, as preliminary to what is to follow in this chapter and the two subsequent ones, that it seems surprising to me that those who call themselves christians, should submit quietly to a state of things—a slavery to fashion—which demands the consumption of nearly the whole amount of the time which God has given us in which to educate ourselves for the great future of this life and the next, in the mere drudgery of the body. We admit in words the inferiority of our animal to our intellectual and moral nature, and yet we spend almost the whole of our waking hours in gratifying the wants of the former; and do it cheerfully. Nay, worse than this, we seem to task our minds and put in requisition to their full extent our inventive powers to devise other luxuries and extravagances, to impel us to greater industry. If by human art the sun could be stopped a few hours in its daily course, so as to give us, every day, as once in the time of Joshua, thirty instead of fifteen hours for labor, the spirit of the age, in its devotion to Fashion, would soon find means to consume all this time on the wants of the perishing body, while the immortal mind and heart might go, as they are now compelled to do, unheeded and neglected.

We are christian in profession, but infidel in practice. We profess to live for the future, while in reality, we live for the present. We compliment knowledge and virtue, and their divine author, while our real sincere homage is rendered to animal pleasure. We talk of heaven, and of having our conversation and thoughts in it, while our affections are of the earth, earthy. We profess to worship God, but we love mammon. We are too much like those of whom it was once said by an inspired man—" whose God is their stomach."

The principles of education—the more important ones I mean—are few and simple. Still, to acquire them in such a manner as to render them useful to us in practice, is not by any means a small matter. It is easy to state some of them, in a work like this; but it is not easy so to state them that they may occupy the same place in other's minds that they do in our own, or have the same relative importance.

I may say, for example, that consistency is one of the great secrets in governing a child; that, however valuable modes or systems are, consistency is more so. But no reader can estimate this principle, as soon as she receives it, just as I do. She needs illustrations of my meaning, by examples of the application and misapplication of the principle; and for these she needs books, and observation, and even experience. And the same is true of any other principle I might advance.

The truth is, that the Creator, for reasons best known to himself, has not permitted us to transmit or receive the opinions, or even the recorded experience of each other entire, in such a way as to make it at once available. Our own minds, like the stomach in the reception of food, must act upon and digest the most enlightened and approved experience ere it becomes our own property. Hence the use of books, which, on the subject of education, should consist chiefly of experience rather than abstract principles; or in which to render them most useful, experience rather than theory should greatly predominate.

CHAPTER XXXIV.

SOCIAL IMPROVEMENT.

Anecdote of Alcibiades. Intention of the Creator. Marriage of course a social state. Morning calls. Evening visits. Excitements. Balls and Theatres. Visiting in the afternoon Social advantages of large families. Visiting by large companies. Topics of conversation. Scandal. Opposition of human nature to the gospel. Reading at social meetings. An important caution.

It is recorded of Alcibiades, that he had the art of conforming himself to the habits, tastes and opinions of whatever company he happened to be in; of "turning either to good or evil with the same facility and ardor, and shifting almost in an instant from one extreme to its opposite." Now what Alcibiades could do in a remarkable degree, almost every individual has the power of doing in a degree greater or less, according to circumstances. Nor is this all. The impression which is made by any company we are in is seldom entirely lost. However unconscious we may be of the fact, we are probably affected, more or less, by every social interview of life.

Nor is this susceptibility of impression to be regretted. The Creator probably intended it as a means of our improvement. It is true, we catch bad habits, manners and opinions, as well as those which are correct; but there is no necessity for this. We are permitted to choose our society. And it is on the wisdom of our choice, for ourselves and for our children, pupils and wards, that much of the good or evil of human society is made to depend. He will be wise—and happy, too—who associates with wise companions; but in the expressive language of the Bible, the companion of fools shall be destroyed.

If these views are correct—and it is presumed no one will doubt their correctness—then we may derive from them two important rules for human conduct. First, that it is our duty, in all the varied circumstances of life, to associate with our fellow creatures; and secondly, that it is our duty to be "wise as serpents" in the selection of our associates.

Of the manner in which children should associate, and of the pains which parents should take in selecting the companions of their sports, studies, &c., it is not my intention, at present, to speak, though they are of unquestionable importance, even to the young wife.

SOCIAL IMPROVEMENT. 329

The circumstance of becoming a wife, ensures at least one important means of social improvement. She who has but one constant associate need not be a hermit. She may make much intellectual and moral progress by this means alone. But she need not and should not confine herself to a circle so narrow. She has relatives and neighbors; perhaps brethren and sisters in the church. These have their claims on her, and she has claims on them. The question at present will be, in what method or methods shall these claims be discharged.

1. Not by morning calls, as they are frequently denominated. I have a most unconquerable aversion to all sorts of "calls," as they are usually made in cities, and populous towns and villages. They seem so hollow and so useless, and such a waste of valuable time, that I wish the whole tribe of them could become extinct.

Morning calls, however, I regard as more objectionable than any other. The morning is the best time for labor, and study, and personal improvement; and some persons are so much accustomed to the good old way of spending the whole of the time before dinner in some one of these employments, that morning calls annoy them exceedingly. A few, it is true, will not suffer themselves to be annoyed in this way; and accordingly they refuse to see any company at this hour, unless on very extraordinary occasions. But others have *nerves*, and are wanting more in moral courage.

If people are careful to rise in proper season, and make a diligent use of all the time till noon, they may then afford to spend some time in social visits. Of the peculiar advantages of afternoon visits, I am to speak presently.

2. Evening visits are, as a general rule, objectionable, especially when begun at a late hour, and attended by a great number of persons. The reasons why this season for visiting is objectionable, I have not room to give, in full. It is sufficient, perhaps, to say, that the evening is usually the best, as it often is the only time of any length, for being alone with our own family—a daily meeting which is indispensable;—that there are many considerations connected with health which are against it, and that it is by no means the most favorable season to morality, and especially to good order.

There are circumstances, however, which render it extremely difficult for some people to find time for visits, as things are, except in the evening. If in such cases a few neighbors choose to meet for conversation in the evening, and retire to their respective homes at an early hour, there can be no very strong objection to the practice; though I think that in the very best state of society, another part of the day would usually be selected.

3. All social interviews in the form of large convivial parties or concerts, are objectionable. Not only are they exciting in their own nature, by the sympathy which large numbers produce, but the excitement is apt to be increased by the use of exciting food or drink. These, it is true, are in some instances banished; and people are beginning to learn that they can be cheerful and happy in each other's society without fermented or alcoholic drinks, and even without tea and coffee, or extra food at extra seasons. Still, however, the multitude of those who have not yet learned this very important lesson is prodigiously great.

They who go much to large evening parties and concerts, are apt to acquire a disrelish for the smaller circles of their own homes. The society of one individual, however much it may at first have been valued, will at length become insipid and monotonous. Why evening parties should have this effect more than parties in the daytime, I will not undertake to determine; but I appeal to every one whose range of observation is extensive, for the truth of the sentiment.

It will scarcely be necessary, after what I have said in this chapter and elsewhere, to inveigh against the practice of attending balls, theatres,

&c. Surely no young wife who values her reputation or that of her family, will be found in the ranks of those who devote their evenings to amusements abroad, in any form—especially to those which are as doubtful in their character and moral tendency, as balls and theatres. Home, in the evening, is the appropriate place for married people, to say nothing of others.

But what then is an appropriate season for social visits ; and what are the most favorable circumstances in which to assemble for social improvement ?

The afternoon, between the hours, say of 3 (provided we have dined at 12) and 7 o'clock, is the best season for visiting, on every account which regards health, economy, or mental or moral culture. This would embrace the usual season for taking the third meal, (or supper, as our plain country people call it,) a point which is believed to be of very great importance ; for though all extra eating and drinking at social visits is to be studiously avoided, it is of much importance that we eat and drink together at appropriate seasons. It is confidently believed that taking our customary meals together, provided these meals are plain and simple, has an effect " to make man mild and sociable to man," which has never been too highly estimated. I would that mankind ate and drank together at their ordinary plain meals, much oftener than they do.

Hence may be seen one reason why I am in favor of having the elder sons, when they can, continue to reside as long as possible under the same roof, and eat at the same table with their aged parents.

The refining and improving effects of eating together, and the economy of the practice—were these alone considered—are believed to be more than sufficient to counterbalance any evils which are supposed to result from it. But this is not all. The great benefit is the daily and sometimes hourly opportunities thus afforded for social improvement of the mind and heart. Such an arrangement of families would do as much towards hastening the millennial glory of the world, as the usual arrangement of society into families as small as possible, does to retard it.

I am not in favor of visiting by very large companies, even when it is done in the afternoon. The smaller the number, in general, the better. When you bring together large numbers, there is so much of art, or rather of formality, as greatly to diminish the tendency to promote real improvement.

The conversation need not be confined to topics of great acknowledged importance. There is no subject on which it is proper to converse publicly at all, which may not be advantageously introduced at these social and neighborly interviews. I have no objection even to politics. Why should not a circle, though it were composed exclusively of females, discuss political questions? Would it not be well for every wife in the United States, to understand such subjects? And if so, are they improper for the social circle? I do not say I would have them enter into these subjects with the fierceness of angry disputants, who have entered the arena of public life in pursuit of a sinecure or a salary. It is one thing to converse calmly and coolly for information, and quite another to dispute sharply; and above all, to dispute for the sake of disputing, or even for the sake of carrying a point.

Nothing is more pleasing than to see a circle of females giving free scope to conversation on the petty as well as larger topics of life, without descending to public or private scandal. Nor is the latter at all necessary, however fashionable.

I do not know that females are more addicted to scandal than males. But there is in both sexes, an unreasonable willingness to hear and even propagate remarks which are unfavorable both to individuals and collective bodies. It is in accordance with human nature, as we usually find it, to speak of the faults of others rather than of their excellencies. The spirit of the Bible requires us to speak of our neighbor's excellencies in his absence, and if he has failings to go and tell him of them privately. But depraved human nature dictates a course exactly the contrary of all this. It seldom leads us to speak of a brother's faults to his face. I might almost say never. And yet we do not hesitate to hold them up, sometimes with ridicule and reproach, to the view of others.

There is another thing to be considered. The more we allow ourselves to dwell on the defects in our neighbor's character, the more those defects rise in magnitude. The more we indulge in unkind feelings towards another, the more unkind do our feelings become. On the contrary, the more we dwell with pleasure on a neighbor's excellencies, the more does our pleasure increase, with respect to him. Let these principles be understood by christians and acted upon, and how would it change the condition of society! And what a powerful agent, in this way, would female social circles be in its transformation!

It is customary at some of our social circles—especially at those fashionable and very interesting meetings in the afternoon, called "sewing circles," to spend a large proportion of the time in mere reading. This does not seem to me at all advisable. Reading may be useful to excite conversation, if it inclines to flag; but I would never use the former as a substitute for the latter. Not because I would not have it a leading object to improve the mind and elevate the heart at these and all other social meetings; but because I think free conversation one of the best means for accomplishing so valuable an end. It is on this account that I have ventured to say that females may even be permitted to converse on politics. I love to see ease and freedom in all this sort of intercourse; but a book appears to cause constraint. The conversation can never indeed be too elevated; the more so the better. I do not contend for the admission of petty topics as a matter of choice, so much as for the sake of freedom. Some of the individuals composing an ordinary social circle, are very far from being literary; and those who are of this description may probably do quite as much good by setting the rest an example of a proper and rational way of conversing on ordinary or petty topics, at least a part of the time, as they could by conversing on more elevated, and, in the abstract, more important subjects.

But while the young wife is seeking to improve her mind and heart by associating often with her neighbors, in one way or another, let her assiduously endeavor to avoid the appearance of aristocracy. There is a most unhappy, I might say unreasonable jealousy of the rich, on the part of the poor; and however conscious the former may be that they do not deserve to be suspected, let them not say that even unfounded and unjust suspicions are to be disregarded. Though fully conscious that they have no aristocratic feelings in their bosoms, let them labor to show their true character by their deeds. Let them be careful to avoid the smallest appearance of evil. Let them select their associates, as much as they may, at all other times; yet, when they have once accepted an invitation to a circle where there are those for whom they have little sympathy, let them, for the time, place themselves on an equal footing with them, and treat them with as much attention as they do others.

There need be no hypocrisy in all this. The Saviour of mankind sometimes associated with publicans and sinners, as well as with other bad people; but will any one suppose, for a moment, that he had a preference, or even a relish, for their society? But he could do them good by it; and that was his object. And he was not afraid of demeaning himself by the course he took. No more should a young wife, who associates for a few hours with persons whose society she would not, in general, prefer. For my own part, I do not believe that the unhappy feeling of the poor towards the rich, which prevails more extensively in this country than many people are aware, and mars the peace and destroys the union of many a church of Christ, will ever be completely removed till some of the disciples of Christ learn more humility and condescension, and endeavor to avoid, not only all evil, but even the appearance of all evil.

CHAPTER XXXV.

MORAL AND RELIGIOUS IMPROVEMENT.

Doing good. Many forms of doing good. Philosophy of doing good. Associated effort. How to select societies. Individual charitable effort. The poor. The ignorant. The vicious. The sick. Caution in regard to visiting the sick. Prayer as a means of improvement. Self-Examination. Reading. The Bible. Other useful books.

ONE means of moral and religious improvement to every individual, whatever may be his professions or relations, is doing good. "It is more blessed to give than to receive," expresses a great truth in relation to this subject; to which representation every one who has watched carefully the operations of his own mind, and studied thoroughly his own character, will cheerfully respond; and the same truth or nearly the same is expressed by the two following passages of scripture:—" He that doeth truth cometh to the light." " If any man will do my will, he shall know of the doctrine whether it be of God."

I do not, of course, mean to say that there is no other source of moral and religious improvement but doing good; but only that doing good is one of the sources—and a never failing one, too—of moral progress; and if our works of love are performed from the sole desire of pleasing God, it can scarcely fail of promoting our religious progress, at the same time.

Of doing good there are many, very many forms. I need not attempt, here, to show that it is not confined to the giving of money; nor indeed to the giving of alms of any sort. Every one knows, or ought to know, that there is a much wider sphere of operation than all this. Indeed, so far as we can judge in a world like this, the giving of money or goods to the poor is usually the least useful charity we can bestow. Much more is done for the permanent relief of individuals or families, when we induce them to be more industrious, more temperate, more pure, more intelligent or more healthful.

Now there are many ways of accomplishing the objects here specified. The truth is, we are so constituted in this world, that what is done for any one individual, let him be ever so mean, is done for the whole. It is like adding a drop to the mighty ocean, which, though it be but a drop, adds to each and every part of the whole expanse. Is it not so? Must it not be so? Precisely thus is it with doing good. Not a particle of the good we do is ever lost. Whether it be done by the young wife to her husband, her family, her domestics, (if she have any,) her friends, her enemies, her neighbors, or the Chinese, makes, in this respect, but little difference. It increases by just so much the great ocean of human good, and enlarges by just so much as it is thus increased, every one's dividend of the whole stock.

Will it be asked how this is done? A full reply to the question would lead me far away from the main subject of the chapter. I should be obliged to go to the scripture for the doctrine of sympathy, of which Paul makes so much. I should be obliged to show, as he has done, only in language far less beautiful and eloquent, that as in the human body, so in human society, taken as a whole, whenever one member suffers, let it be ever so apparently insignificant a member, all the rest of the members suffer with it ; and whenever one member rejoices, all the other members rejoice with it. I should be obliged to treat at large, by a reference to every one's observation and to history, on the dealings of Divine Providence with the great human family. And, lastly, I should perhaps, to complete the argument, be obliged to enter upon a lengthy appeal to your own understandings on the very nature of the case; in other words, endeavor to show that the doctrine is one which approves itself to the sober dictates of common sense.

Let us therefore, for the present, take it for granted. Let us believe, if we can, that no particle of good which is done is ever lost; nay, that the condition of every intelligent being is really, though from its minuteness it may be imperceptibly, improved by it. How will such a belief strengthen the hand and warm the heart!

Many a young wife, removed, perhaps, from the circle in which she has been accustomed to move, and left comparatively alone, excepting the society of her husband, is ready to ask, what good she can do. Now all I hope to do, at the present time, is to show her that as long as she has a single rational being within her reach, she has the means of doing good—as much so, though not exactly in the same way, as the missionary to China or Hawaii; and that if she makes her husband truly and really happier in any way than he would otherwise have been, whether it be by enlightening his mind, warming his heart—whether by words, actions or mere looks—she not only does him good, but does good, in strictness of philosophical and Bible language, to the most distant savage of New Holland or the South Sea; and lastly, that whenever a particle of good is thus done, it promotes, in a greater or less degree, her own moral progress;—that, in short, she is not only bound by the laws of the great Creator to every other part and portion of his moral world, but that she cannot move a step or lift a finger, strictly speaking, without affecting,* either beneficially or otherwise, the whole of it.

How does this view of things enhance the value of female effort! What individual, either married or single, who receives it, can longer complain of being a cypher in the world! How can she who has a husband, a brother, a sister, a father, a mother, a cousin, a neighbor even, want for opportunities of usefulness, and consequently for the means of moral and religious progress!

I have elsewhere spoken of doing good by association. This in modern times has become very

---

* Perhaps this view might have been rendered more intelligible by the following illustration:—Every one knows that the earth, by a general law, attracts the sun, to a limited extent, as truly as the sun attracts the earth. But if so, if the whole attracts, then each part of which the whole is composed has a share in the work of attraction, and has its sphere of influence.—Just so I judge it to be in the moral world. Every particle of moral good has its sphere of attraction and repulsion, and may be said to have its own appropriate relations to every other particle; and he who can add to the sum total of moral good, in the least conceivable degree, adds to the stock of each individual's happiness, taking into consideration his whole existence, both here and hereafter.

fashionable, and woman, warm hearted as she usually is, has caught the spirit. This is matter of joy rather than of regret, provided her associated efforts are well directed, and are not allowed to interfere with the duties which devolve upon her as an individual.

But let us then take it for granted, that woman has leisure in which she may properly step aside and do something in the way of voluntary associations. The claims of a number of associations present themselves. From these she will probably select such as are most congenial to her feelings, and best adapted to her circumstances. To such she will, it is hoped, for the time be faithful. Nothing is more foolish, in my opinion, in either sex, than a desire to become mere nominal members of a great many societies. It is worse than useless; it is a moral wrong. If we join a society, we ought to feel ourselves morally obligated to attend its meetings, and by our presence, our advice, our efforts—our money, if necessary—help forward its operations. If we do this, and do it from a right principle, it will most unquestionably conduce greatly to our moral and religious progress and improvement.

Yet, after every effort of this kind, there will still remain a wide field for doing good as individuals, to those who are around us. There are in almost every neighborhood, the poor, or the ignorant, or the vicious, or the sick. All these are often within the reach of the voluntary efforts of any charitable individual.

She may find employment for the poor, or at least she can make the attempt. She has "her reward," even if she fails. Or if she can do no more, she can see and sympathize with them; for even this will warm her heart and accelerate her progress in the path of virtue and piety.

She may instruct the ignorant, or at least cause them to be instructed. There are many ways of doing this. She may do it by inducing parents to send them to school—to the infant, district, or Sabbath school. She may do it by giving them books or tracts, or by inducing them to buy them. She may do it by conversation, both with parents and with children.

She may reclaim the vicious—at least she may hope to do something towards it. It is doing something toward this to find them employment, and to provide for their instruction.

But there is no office in which woman appears more like an angel, than when she is found visiting and relieving, or endeavoring to relieve the sick or the afflicted, and pouring into their minds and hearts, the oil and wine of consolation. Sympathy with the sick is a duty which is too often withheld,

It is often said that if we cannot do the sick any good, it is best not to go near them. I grant it. But we can do them good. We often do them a great deal of good simply by letting it be known that we take the pains to inquire after them.

I am not at all in favor of injuring the sick by useless or worse than useless visits. Everything should be under the direction of the physician. Many a sick person has been hastened out of the world by our presence and anxieties, when our services were not wanted. But it is easy to call and inquire of the friends how the sick do, without going near them; and it is easy to inform the sick that such and such individuals make inquiries and take a deep interest in them, without frightening them by it. On the contrary, if done properly, it will generally increase their cheerfulness, their courage, and their hopes—and this, if it can be done without too much expense, always does good. Multitudes might be saved by our sympathies, as well as by our money, or our more direct personal efforts.

In short, the way to do good in this world is exceedingly broad. I have, in these remarks, merely glanced at it. Let it not be said, that I involve myself in a contradiction, and say at one time that home is the province of women, while at others, I would send her abroad half her time, on works of charity. All I mean to say is, that if woman has not enough to do at home, or thinks she has not, there is no occasion for sitting down in inaction, or wasting her conversation or her strength in a way which will not only fail to promote her happiness or her piety, but will jeopardize if not gradually destroy both.

But though I estimate benevolent action as a means of self-improvement very highly, it is very far from being the only or the principal means of moral and religious progress. I need not surely remind the reader of the tendency of prayer to this end, since I conceive it to be so intimately connected with charitable efforts, that the one usually accompanies the other. True it is, that we may give all our goods to feed the poor, as Paul has expressed it, and yet be destitute of genuine love to God and man; but I have been taking my reader to possess this love or charity in the first place, and to be moved by it to action; and if thus moved, I still say that the benevolent efforts of the individual will, almost inevitably, be accompanied by prayer. Who can labor daily and assiduously for the improvement of a husband or any other dear relation, and not at the same time pray for him? Who can join in the cause of temperance or moral reform and not pray? Who can visit the abodes of ignorance, and vice, and disease, and not be often at the throne of divine grace, pleading for wisdom to direct in every effort for their removal?

The bare mention of prayer, in a work like this, will doubtless disturb some of the fastidious, and lead them to cry out, bigotry. On this point, there are individuals among us who might take a hint from the Mohammedans. When some of the ladies of the ship Delaware—so we are told by Mr. Jones, in his excursions to Cairo, Jerusalem, &c.— were admitted to the harem of the Pasha of Egypt, at Cairo, they found that their presence did not hinder the sultana from retiring at the exact time for prayers. Such is the strictness of the Mohammedans in this matter; and yet christians are almost ashamed to speak of prayer, or have others do it, lest they should be thought superstitious or bigoted.

Nor is self-examination of less importance, in its place, than prayer. It was a sacred rule with the Pythagoreans, every evening to think over, three times, the events of the day; and it would be well if christians were equally attentive to a duty which is as important and useful now, as it was two or three thousand years ago. How much the habit of self-examination conduces to our improvement can never be known, or indeed imagined, by those who have not tried it. Indeed, it is difficult to conceive how one can be a christian, or esteem herself so, who neglects so important a duty. Happy is she whose habits are in this respect what they should be! And happier still the husband and wife, who, in addition to their duties to themselves, separately, have their stated daily seasons for mutual free conversation, suggestion and correction. What an important aid would this be, to progress in the path of the just towards that world, to which, by the eye of faith, they are looking!

Lastly, much moral and religious aid may be derived from books. Of these, the first in importance is the Bible. The claims of this book, independent of the consideration that it is divinely inspired, are exceedingly high. It is full of human nature; and they who wish to study themselves, or to rise above their present condition and advance towards the purer region of the perfect, should make it a daily counsellor. It is not the language of mere compliment when we speak of its superiority. Men of mere literary taste, who cared very little for its divine origin or inspiration, have testified the same thing concerning it. They say that, viewed as a mere work of human composition, there is nothing like it. I beg the young wife to study— above all other books—this interesting and all-important volume.

Next to this, perhaps, comes Watts' "Improvement of the Mind." This is a most splendid production, and will stand as a monument of the piety as well as talent of the writer, while time shall last. There are many more valuable treatises in our libraries, among which are Mason on Self-Knowledge, Degerando on Self-Education, and Doddridge's Rise and Progress of Religion. These works alone are a host; and carefully read and studied, can scarcely fail to bring forth the most valuable fruits.

CHAPTER XXXVI.

MORAL INFLUENCE ON THE HUSBAND.

Mode of female influence on the husband Mr. Flint's encomium. Examples of female influence. Wife of Jonathan Edwards—of Sir James Mackintosh. True position of woman in society. Serious error of some modern writers. A caution. Making haste to be rich. A species of mania. Its extent and evils. How the young wife is concerned with it. What she can do to remove it. Agur's prayer—seldom used in modern times. Particular modes of female influence. Office seeking. How to dissuade from it. Exposures to intemperance. Female consistency. Female piety. Its effects on the husband—compared with amiableness and beauty. Apparent objection to the writer's views. Woman's prerogative.

EVERY wife has it in her power to make her husband either better or worse. This result is accomplished, not merely by giving advice, nor by advice and instruction alone. Both these have their influence; and as means of improvement, should not be neglected. But it is by the general tone and spirit of her conversation, as manifesting the temper and disposition of the heart, that she makes the most abiding impressions. These are modifying his character daily and hourly; sometimes even when absent. The thought of what a wife wishes or expects, especially when a letter or paper is occasionally received from her or from some member of the family, is silently and perhaps unconsciously changing a husband's character.

So obvious is this, that it has become a matter of common observation. Every one is ready to observe the change produced in a husband by a second marriage. Now is it probable that this change is greater than that which was produced in him at the first marriage, except that in the second case it is less expected, and there are more interested observers? And yet it is so great as to have led to the very general belief that stepmothers have an uncommon—I was going to say a sort of magic—influence.

It is by no means denied that the influence, in the matrimonial state, is reciprocal. No doubt it is. But I am not writing now for husbands, directly. Besides, however great may be the changes wrought in the wife by the husband, those which are wrought in the latter by the wife are frequently more surprising as well as more permanent.

But if it be true that woman is thus silently changing the current of man's affections, and the tenor of his thoughts and habits, how important that she should be well taught! How worthy of consideration the claims which have been urged in the preceding pages, and the motives which I have endeavored to present for her improvement! And how important—nay, how just—in this point of view, was the remark of Mr. Flint, in one of the numbers of the Western Review—" If this world," said he, " is ever to become a better and a happier world, woman, properly educated and truly benevolent, sensible of her influence and wise enough to exert it aright, must be the original mover in the great work."

"I tremble for the man who does not tremble for himself," was once said in reference to the temptations which exist in this country of abundance, to become intemperate. In like manner, I tremble for the woman who, in view of the nature and extent of her influence on man—and primarily on her husband and family—does not tremble, lest it should not be so good an influence as it ought to be—such, indeed, as she may wish a thousand ages hence it had been. It is truly a solemn subject, and I envy not those who can make light of it. They will not make light of it when standing by the bed of death, or when their own hour of dissolution has arrived. They will not make light of it when they stand in the judgment, or when they come to inhabit eternity.

It has been said of the wife of Jonathan Edwards, that by enabling him to put forth his powers unembarrassed, she conferred a greater benefit upon mankind, than all the female public characters that ever lived or ever will live. A similar remark might be applied to the mother of almost every great and good man. Woman's true greatness consists, so it seems to me, in rendering others useful, rather than in being directly useful herself. Or, in other words, it is less her office to be seen and known in society, than to make others seen and known, and their influence felt.

I might give numerous examples and illustrations of the principle I am endeavoring to sustain, both in this country and elsewhere. I might speak of the mother and the wife of Washington, of the mother of Dwight, Franklin, Wilberforce, Whitefield, Timothy, and hundreds of others; for it was by the exercise of the duties not only of the mother, but of the wife, that these illustrious characters were brought forth to the world. But I will confine myself to a single instance; and that one in which the influence upon the husband was direct.

The case to which I refer, is that of Sir James Mackintosh, whose fame as a jurist, a statesman and a writer is well known, not only in Europe and America, but in India; and whose efforts in the cause of science and humanity have rarely been equalled. Few men have done more, in the progress of a long life, than he; and few have, at any rate, been more distinguished for extensive learning, large views, and liberal principles, in law, politics and philosophy; but especially in his favorite department of the law. It was he of whom Sir Walter Scott said, on a certain occasion, that he made "the most brilliant speech ever made, at bar, or in forum." Yet this great man, if we may believe his own story, owed no small share of his greatness to the assistance and influence of his wife. Of this the following extract from a letter of his to a friend, describing her character, after her decease, will most abundantly prove. The last clause includes, it will be seen, a passing tribute to another person—probably his mother—which doubles the value of the extract I have made in exhibiting the influence of two females in the formation of character, instead of but one.

"Allow me, in justice to her memory, to tell you what she was, and what I owed her. I was guided in my choice only by the blind affection of my youth. I found an intelligent companion, and a tender friend, a prudent monitress, the most faithful of wives, and a mother as tender as children ever had the misfortune to lose. I met a woman who, by the tender management of my weaknesses, gradually corrected the most pernicious of them. She became prudent from affection; and though of the most generous nature, she was taught frugality and economy by her love for me.

"During the most critical period of my life, she preserved order in my affairs, from the care of which she relieved me. She gently reclaimed me from dissipation; she propped my weak and irresolute nature; she urged my indolence to all the exertions that have been useful or creditable to me, and she was perpetually at hand to admonish my heedlessness and improvidence. To her I owe whatever I am; to her, whatever I shall be. In her solicitude for my interest, she never for a moment forgot my feelings or my character. Even in her occasional resentments, for which I but too often gave her cause, (would to God I could recall those moments,) she had no sullenness or acrimony. Her feelings were warm and impetuous, but she was placable, tender and constant.

"Such was she whom I have lost; and I have lost her when her excellent natural sense was rapidly improving, after eight years of struggle and distress had bound us fast to each other—when a knowledge of her worth had refined my youthful love into friendship, before age had deprived it of much of its original ardor. I lost her, alas, (the choice of my youth and the partner of my misfortunes,) at a moment when I had a prospect of her sharing my better days.

"The philosophy which I have learnt, only teaches me that virtue and friendship are the greatest of human blessings, and that their loss is irreparable. It aggravates my calamity, instead of consoling me under it. My wounded heart seeks another consolation. Governed by these feelings, which have in every age and region of the world actuated the human mind, I seek relief, and I find it, in the soothing hope and consolatory opinion, that a benevolent wisdom inflicts the chastisements, as well as bestows the enjoyments of human life; that superintending goodness will one day enlighten the darkness which surrounds our nature, and hangs over our prospects; that this dreary and wretched life is not the whole of man; that an animal so sagacious and provident, and capable of such proficiency in science and virtue, is not like the beasts that perish; that there is a dwelling place prepared for the spirits of the just, and that the ways of God will yet be vindicated to man. The sentiments of religion, which were implanted in my mind in my early youth, and which were revived by the awful scenes which I have seen passing before my eyes in the world, are I trust deeply rooted in my heart by this great calamity."

Who—what wife, especially—can read these paragraphs, without feeling a desire enkindled within her to be distinguished in the world, not so much in her own name as by her influence on her husband and family, and through them on others? She thus becomes not so much the instrument of human amelioration, as the moving agent.

But a little explanation may be desirable. I am not inculcating Mohammedan or Pagan notions in regard to woman. I still insist on her having a distinct character; and no one is more forward than myself in opposing the idea of her merging her own individuality in that of her husband. I insist on her forming for herself a character quite independent of his; and a perfect one, too. In becoming a wife, I say again, no individual is to dispossess herself of any trait of character which was hers before. She is still an independent woman, notwithstanding: just as I am none the less an independent man, by becoming a member of some association. My new character and the new duties are superinduced—added to the duties which existed before. In the same way we lose nothing—dispossess ourselves of nothing—when we form new relations. No person is the less a brother, a sister, a child, a neighbor, or a citizen, because he or she has entered into the bonds of matrimony. New duties are indeed added, and new obligations imposed; but the old ones remain. We have, in effect, so many different characters to sustain; and marriage only adds one—though a very important one—to the number already existing. The wife, in becoming one with her husband, and forming, in one point of view, a new and more perfect character, loses nothing, of necessity, of her individuality; nor does her husband. Nay, more—much more than all this—the latter is, or at least ought to become so much the more perfect by it.

Perhaps, after all, there is nothing peculiar in the sentiments I have advanced; but as the language was open to a little misconstruction, it was thought desirable to render it as intelligible as possible. The necessity for doing this, seemed to me to be greater, in consequence of the efforts which have been made, for some time past, to encourage woman, either directly or indirectly, to think more of her individual influence, both literary and political.

I do not know that any direct attempts have been made to disparage woman, as a wife and as a mother, but such has been the tendency of things, indirectly. Hannah More, and Felicia Hemans, and Harriet Martineau, and Miss Somerville are lauded, not so much because they are excellent wives, mothers, daughters or sisters, as because they are excellent poets, moralists, or mathematicians ; and it has been publicly asserted as a blessing to the world, that Hannah More never entered into married life! As if her labors, valuable as they are, would bear, for one moment, a comparison with those of the wife of Jonathan Edwards or James Mackintosh.

Nor is this all. It is not men alone who have complimented the aspirations of the other sex to literary or political fame. Females themselves are beginning to make claims. " Henceforth," says Miss Martineau, " when men fire at the name of Flora McIvor, let women say—There will be more Floras when women feel that they have political power and duties."

The truth is, that these characters, however valuable to the world they may be, would be more valuable if more devoted to their appropriate sphere. But has not the custom of lauding to the skies such individuals, while thousands in useful domestic life have been overlooked and forgotten, been one reason why so many young females of the present day have such aversion to the kitchen, and gravely tell us they would almost as soon die as have their hands employed in dish water?

MORAL INFLUENCE ON THE HUSBAND.

Having thus expressed my views, in a general way, I may now be allowed to enter into a little more of detail. My object will be to mention a few particulars in which the young wife's influence on her husband will be especially valuable.

Most men are too much devoted to money-making. Nor is this the worst. They are not merely desirous of becoming wealthy, in a reasonable time and in proportion to their own diligent efforts; for were it so, the evil would be more tolerable. But they are *in haste to be rich.*

There was a period in the history of our country, especially of the New England division of it, when a few individuals might be found who could join in the prayer of Agur—" Give me neither poverty nor riches." But how strangely are the times altered! Where is now the man who can, from the heart, utter this prayer? Where is he whose prayer is not—I do not say his words, but his real prayer, his *desire*—Give me riches; and give it to me immediately: I cannot wait.

Once it was only a few individuals in the community who could hope to acquire wealth, unless born to its possession. There were few Solomons or Crœsuses. It is even so now, in some parts of the world. The nobles are comparatively few. But what was once the sin of the prince or the tyrant who controlled the community, is now the sin of nearly every individual composing it. Especially is this true of the community in which we live. The matter of liberty has indeed descended to us from our fathers ; but for what ? What, indeed, but that we may use our liberty in making haste to be rich—and in taking every advantage of doing this which the letter of the law, or of public sentiment, which is nearly the same thing, does not positively prohibit?

Hence the spirit of *speculation*, which everywhere prevails, and which has even seized on the hearts of many who profess to be governed by better motives. I fear there are some professing christians who do not hesitate to enter into any sort of speculation which the public sentiment does not denounce, provided they have a strong hope of filling their pockets by it.

The following sentiments, from the editor of a paper in this city, so well express my own views on this subject, that I have obtained leave to copy them for this place :

"We do not mean to be understood, in our remarks, as censuring the ordinary exchange of one commodity for another, at a reasonable profit, but that grasping after enormous advances, and profits in trade, by which men are continually making haste to be rich. How variously this unhallowed spirit has developed itself within a few years past, let the history of those years tell. It is enough to say, that money, lands, houses and merchandize have all been subjected to this unnatural and unholy mode of transfer, until speculation has almost usurped the place of honest trade. Thousands have left a respectable calling, in which they were reasonably prosperous, to embark in speculation; and many of them have been ruined by it. They made haste to be rich.

"It is a lamentable truth, that professing christians have extensively engaged in this species of gambling. One of the great evils which results from this unholy love of gain, is, that it secularizes the feelings of those engaged in it, and thus becomes an opposing principle of the gospel; the object of which is, to destroy the worldliness of the heart, and make it spiritual and heavenly. This secular spirit is brought into the church; it pervades its councils, and throws its influence over the body of worshipping saints. A few who breathe it, soon bring the feelings and policy of that branch of the church with which they are connected, to a perfect conformity with their own; and a system of worldly wisdom and prudence takes the place of the gospel rule of duty, while *faith* and *humility* are trampled in the dust.

"All the love of God which has shed itself abroad in the hearts of his children, all the mercy which gathered like a halo around the cross of Christ, all the incentives to hope and gratitude which eternity unfolds, as well as the terrors of the second death itself, have been unavailing to induce men, and even professing christians too, to relinquish their grasp upon earthly things, or banish from their hearts the unhallowed love of gain.

"What a spectacle is here presented. A community which owes its existence to, and professes to derive its support from certain spiritual truths, obsequiously bows itself down to the government of worldly maxims; and meanly submits to be directed by the art and cunning of unsanctified men. But this is, and ever must be the result, when those upon whom are the vows of God, make haste to be rich.

"The effect is, if possible, worse on individual minds, than on the body of the church. Not only does the watchfulness and anxiety, the bustle and confusion, attendant upon speculation, clash with the peaceful spirit of piety, but the heart thus accustomed to worldliness, becomes indurated with it; and when the effect is once produced, powerful indeed must that influence be, which can soften and mould into the image of God, the petrified soul. With how little weight does the word of the Lord come upon the ear of such a man. Accustomed mostly to instruments conveying property or securing it, the awful truths of the Bible cease to have their own simple, native force upon the mind. Speculation destroys the moral sense; shuts up the avenues of the soul; and encases it in an armor, which is proof against the shafts of spiritual truth.

"And while it does this, it at the same time takes the christian from his place by the throne, and bears him where his feeble voice cannot reach the Almighty. It shuts up the way to the mercy seat. How can any man confide in Christ, while the fact flashes full in his face, that he walks by sight and not by faith? How can he believe, while he knows he is daily disobeying that command of God—"Lay not up for yourselves treasures upon earth?" How can he have access to the Father, while he knows his whole life is the opposite of the apostles, who looked not upon the things which are seen, but upon those which are unseen? As the spirit of speculation hinders access to the throne in prayer, and shuts up all the avenues to the soul, how soon does the light of God become extinct in the heart."

Is it asked how this concerns the young wife? Surely such a question is not necessary. Has she no influence in continuing this lamentable state of things? On the contrary, is it not in her power to extend and promote, or to limit and even to suppress it, at her option? Has God given her the power to mould the character of her husband almost as she will, and has she no sort of control over his love for making money?

That it may require a great deal of time to turn the current of thought in a worldly young man—such as most young men are supposed to be, at marriage, and give it a more rational direction, is most true; but that it cannot be done at all, no one will pretend who has the least knowledge of human nature as it is, or of the motives which govern human action. And when I see a man go on from the day of his marriage to the end of life, in one continued series of effort to lay up property, as the principal object worth possessing, and when, above all, I see aged men, like aged trees,

"Strike deeper and cling closer their vile roots,
Still more enamored of this wretched soil,"

I cannot forbear to conclude that no effort has been made, worth the name, to prevent such a state of things, and to *fear* that the mania has possessed not only the husband, but also the wife.

The last suggestion—suspicion rather—may be revolting to some minds. Female avarice is, I confess, particularly shocking. But such a thing there is, shocking as it may be. There are females, there are wives even, to be found, not a whit less avaricious than their husbands. For the honor of human nature, however, we may hope their number is not large.

There is a class of persons in society, who, though they see and feel the enormity of the evil I have mentioned, do yet, in their ignorance, sustain and encourage it. Nor is their number very small, either. Tell them this, and they will shudder. And yet nothing can be more true, as I shall now endeavor to show.

These individuals may possibly think they can say, with Agur—Give me neither poverty nor riches. They may suppose they only desire a competence. But their ideas of what constitutes a competence differ greatly from Agur's. Besides, I doubt whether they really believe they could utter—from the heart—his prayer. They probably believe, as is the more general belief, that riches are in themselves a blessing. What they shudder at, is the idea of being so devoted to them as to take wrong, or at least unchristian methods to procure them. Against these, they would protest; and against these they may not fail, from time to time, to caution their husbands. They will do it, moreover, in the sincerity of their hearts. They regard an over-anxiety to get or lay up money as not only abhorrent in the sight of God, but absolutely vulgar.

Such, I say, are their feelings when they contemplate the subject of buying, and selling, and laboring, merely to get gain. That is, in the abstract, they disapprove of avarice altogether, and they do not hesitate to beg their husbands never to fall under its influence.

Now I hardly need repeat here, what has been more than once insisted on already, that it is not our precepts that form character so much, even in the relation of husband and wife, and parent and child, as our example. It is the spirit which we manifest; the tone of our conversation; the language of our looks, habits and actions.

A young wife says to her husband—and in sincerity, too, no doubt—I hope you will not enter into any sort of speculation, or run any large risks, like Mr. T. and Gen. L. Do let us be contented with a small income; and if Providence gives us more than we need, we know of charitable uses enough to which we can apply it. I do hope, moreover, you will not make a slave of yourself. After being employed a reasonable number of hours daily, it is your duty—and I need not tell you how much it will contribute to your own happiness, and the happiness of others—to spend the rest of your time with your family—conversing with and instructing them, and occasionally visiting your neighbors.

But of how little avail is such language, when she seizes on every convenient occasion to speak in the highest terms of Mr. T.'s beautiful house, and furniture, and garden, and grounds, and of his elegant horses and carriages, and convenient *help*; and contrasts these often with their own? Or when she speaks often of Gen. L.'s industrious habits, commends him for his thrift, and says it is doubtless owing, in part, to the fact that he is constantly in the shop from five o'clock in the morning till nine at night—is not her meaning obvious? Does any husband, who is not an idiot, misunderstand such language? And when it is reiterated from day to day, when it is introduced with greater ease, dwelt upon with greater pleasure, and continued longer than almost any other topic of conversation, must it not have a powerful influence upon him?

He loves his wife, and loves to see her happy. And though he may disapprove of her devotion to externals, yet he finds her high estimation of them has become inwoven, as it were, in her very constitution; and though he labors zealously to remove it, he finds, to his regret, that early impressions on this subject, as well as on most others, are with very great difficulty effaced.

Actions, it is said, speak louder than words. A female may show what her inclinations are in regard to houses, furniture, equipage, servants, food, dress, &c., without saying much about them. Most husbands know enough of the character of their wives to know on what their hearts are set, without the assistance even of language.

But it is in vain for the wife to say one thing, while in her heart she means another. Her good counsels, like the foregoing, cannot have a very deep or lasting effect, while the husband perceives, as clearly as he sees the sun at noon-day, that though she thinks she despises wealth, in the abstract, she fondly hankers after that which wealth alone can procure or enable her to use. And is there any doubt in regard to the course of conduct which, under such circumstances, he will pursue?

Should these thoughts meet the eye of any individual who is thus unconsciously luring her husband along the downward road to misery, and robbing herself and others of the pleasure and advantages of his society in the journey of life, I beg her to stop and reflect before she goes farther. Let her consider, I say, her own present happiness and the happiness of those around her; but what is of still more importance, let her cast a thought forward to the great future, and consider what will be the consequences of this love of possession, not to one or two or half a dozen persons, but to great multitudes, hundreds of ages hence. Let her, in one word, try to form some correct notion of the nature and extent of human responsibility.

Not a few young husbands, in a country where all may aspire to the highest offices, will be found on the list of office-seekers. Now advice here may be less necessary to the wife than on most other subjects; and yet who shall say that she is in no danger of falling short of her duty, and even of her own ultimate wishes, in the course she may be led to pursue?

She does not indeed advise him to seek to be distinguished in this way; for she cares less about state or national affairs, in themselves considered, than we may sometimes suppose. There is certainly something true in the saying of a learned physiologist, that with woman "a man"—her husband especially—"is more than a nation;" by which is meant, not that she is totally regardless of national affairs, but that her husband and his respectability at home are everything to her, comparatively speaking, and the nation only a secondary matter.

And yet, as a means of attaining to that felicity which they suppose a certain condition in regard to externals will procure, there are not a few excellent women who will not only refrain from discouraging their husbands in the pursuit, but will even encourage them, at least indirectly, in their efforts at distinction.

Now let that female who is not only willing but anxious that her husband should obtain an office and a salary, remember that almost all civil offices in this country are very dearly bought. Let her refrain from encouraging what may at best prove a snare—morally—to all who are or may be concerned in the results. Let her not only do this, but let her make every reasonable effort to discourage an inordinate degree of ambition, by turning his thoughts into some other more favorable and useful channel.

But as I have said in relation to the mania for money-making, so I say in regard to office-seeking— it will be of comparatively little use to talk to a husband against the folly or wickedness of seeking office, while you show, plainly, if it be only by your eye and the tone of your voice, that you are deeply interested in the external circumstances of Mr. B.'s family, since they came into the possession of a salary. You must first purify your own heart; for it is out of the abundance of the heart that the mouth speaketh; and if the heart is inclined to parade, it will not fail to show itself, though you may not go so far as to say a single word on the subject.

Perhaps your husband is in danger of intemperance, or you fear he is. He stops occasionally at doubtful places, or falls in occasionally with doubtful company. Will you therefore rate or scold him? Can you do more than to make home as agreeable as possible, and allure him to it by your cheerful, sprightly conversation, your love of study, and your fondness for his society in preference to that of all others?

I have said enough elsewhere of the importance of making your husband's home a happy one—a scene of the purest pleasure and the most exalted improvement. If this point is not gained, remember that nothing is gained. All else goes for nothing, while home is not pleasant, and while one regards it as but doing penance to be there.

In short, unless you love your husband as you ought, and have caught the spirit of improvement, you will never succeed in finding anything worthy the name of happiness below the sun. But with this love and this spirit, and a good fund of plain common sense, you will not, you cannot fail to be happy. With this, all external circumstances will be pleasant—at least comparatively so. Life will be such as will be likely to secure life's great end; and death will be but the door to a better and more enduring state of happiness.

I cannot close without saying a few words in regard to one thing of which I may not yet have spoken with sufficient plainness. I allude to personal piety. The desire for improvement must include the desire of being everything which God made us to be, and of rendering others such, or it falls far short of its highest object.

Is there anything which can ornament female character, whether in the single or the married state, but especially the latter, like deep, heart-felt, practical piety? What like this can make woman, frail as she is, so much like an angel on earth? What, like this, can render the vale of tears she is destined to pass, in any tolerable degree comfortable? Amiableness, in all its forms, is attractive and lovely; especially when accompanied by a well-cultivated and well-balanced mind. Yet what is it without piety?

The same remarks may be made, and with still greater force, in regard to beauty. This, when accompanied by a refined mind, is almost irresistible. Yet what is it without piety? Dr. Young says that wit without sense is worse than nothing; since it only "hoists more sail to run against a rock." So is it—or rather much worse—with beauty, when alone. It serves but to foster weakness, vanity and pride, and to become a lure to a species of idolatry—the worshipping of self.

Such, I may again say, is human nature, that without piety its evil qualities are ever ready to break out in their worst shapes. Amiableness has its charms—beauty too is charming—and virtue is above both; but piety excels them all. Piety is like a diamond in the midst of pearls. It is a sun, that enlivens, cheers and warms all around it.

All that I have thus said would apply to the female in every condition of human life; but it is especially applicable to the wife. It is so in every point of view which concerns herself. It is so, also, in reference to the influence she is to exert upon her husband.

Is it too much to say, that every wife holds, in this respect, an almost absolute power over her husband? Is it too much to say, that the influence of her example is beyond the power of human calculation? Is it beyond the truth to say, that piety in a young wife, who is truly beloved, is irresistible?

And yet all husbands, it will be said, are not pious, even though they have pious wives. True; but all husbands do not love their wives. There is much of marrying for other and more ignoble purposes than genuine affection, or even solid esteem.

There is, however, another consideration. All wives are not pious who seem to be. We must be cautious, therefore, about deciding on the inefficiency of true piety, when embodied in constant and consistent female example. Have we full evidence that such preaching—where true affection is not a stranger—was ever permanently and successfully resisted during the whole of a long life? On the contrary, do not the numerous examples of reformation which exist where female piety, impressed by consistent example, and recommended by the most tender love, allow us to infer, that, if not absolutely irresistible, it is little short of it?

Has the influence of woman in the work of human redemption, received the attention which it deserves, even from christians? Her agency in the fall is duly acknowledged, and perhaps duly felt. But is it not the proud prerogative of the pious wife to be as efficient in the work of restoring, as she was in the work of ruining the race? Is she second to any but the christian minister in the great work of an educator—in the sacred employment of elevating the noble part of man, and directing it to the blissful abodes for which it was originally created?

Family in America

AN ARNO PRESS / NEW YORK TIMES COLLECTION

Abbott, John S. C. **The Mother at Home:** Or, The Principles of Maternal Duty. 1834.

Abrams, Ray H., editor. **The American Family in World War II.** 1943.

Addams, Jane. **A New Conscience and an Ancient Evil.** 1912.

The Aged and the Depression: Two Reports, 1931–1937. 1972.

Alcott, William A. **The Young Husband.** 1839.

Alcott, William A. **The Young Wife.** 1837.

American Sociological Society. **The Family.** 1909.

Anderson, John E. **The Young Child in the Home.** 1936.

Baldwin, Bird T., Eva Abigail Fillmore and Lora Hadley. **Farm Children.** 1930.

Beebe, Gilbert Wheeler. **Contraception and Fertility in the Southern Appalachians.** 1942.

Birth Control and Morality in Nineteenth Century America: Two Discussions, 1859–1878. 1972.

Brandt, Lilian. **Five Hundred and Seventy-Four Deserters and Their Families.** 1905. Baldwin, William H. **Family Desertion and Non-Support Laws.** 1904.

Breckinridge, Sophonisba P. **The Family and the State:** Select Documents. 1934.

Calverton, V. F. **The Bankruptcy of Marriage.** 1928.

Carlier, Auguste. **Marriage in the United States.** 1867.

Child, [Lydia]. **The Mother's Book.** 1831.

Child Care in Rural America: Collected Pamphlets, 1917–1921. 1972.

Child Rearing Literature of Twentieth Century America, 1914–1963. 1972.

The Colonial American Family: Collected Essays, 1788–1803. 1972.

Commander, Lydia Kingsmill. **The American Idea.** 1907.

Davis, Katharine Bement. **Factors in the Sex Life of Twenty-Two Hundred Women.** 1929.

Dennis, Wayne. **The Hopi Child.** 1940.

Epstein, Abraham. **Facing Old Age.** 1922. New Introduction by Wilbur J. Cohen.

The Family and Social Service in the 1920s: Two Documents, 1921–1928. 1972.

Hagood, Margaret Jarman. **Mothers of the South.** 1939.

Hall, G. Stanley. **Senescence:** The Last Half of Life. 1922.

Hall, G. Stanley. **Youth:** Its Education, Regimen, and Hygiene. 1904.

Hathway, Marion. **The Migratory Worker and Family Life.** 1934.

Homan, Walter Joseph. **Children & Quakerism.** 1939.

Key, Ellen. **The Century of the Child.** 1909.

Kirchwey, Freda. **Our Changing Morality:** A Symposium. 1930.

Kopp, Marie E. **Birth Control in Practice.** 1934.

Lawton, George. **New Goals for Old Age.** 1943.

Lichtenberger, J. P. **Divorce:** A Social Interpretation. 1931.

Lindsey, Ben B. and Wainwright Evans. **The Companionate Marriage.** 1927. New Introduction by Charles Larsen.

Lou, Herbert H. **Juvenile Courts in the United States.** 1927.

Monroe, Day. **Chicago Families.** 1932.

Mowrer, Ernest R. **Family Disorganization.** 1927.

Reed, Ruth. **The Illegitimate Family in New York City.** 1934.

Robinson, Caroline Hadley. **Seventy Birth Control Clinics.** 1930.

Watson, John B. **Psychological Care of Infant and Child.** 1928.

White House Conference on Child Health and Protection. **The Home and the Child.** 1931.

White House Conference on Child Health and Protection. **The Adolescent in the Family.** 1934.

Young, Donald, editor. **The Modern American Family.** 1932.

Soc
HQ
759
A4
1972

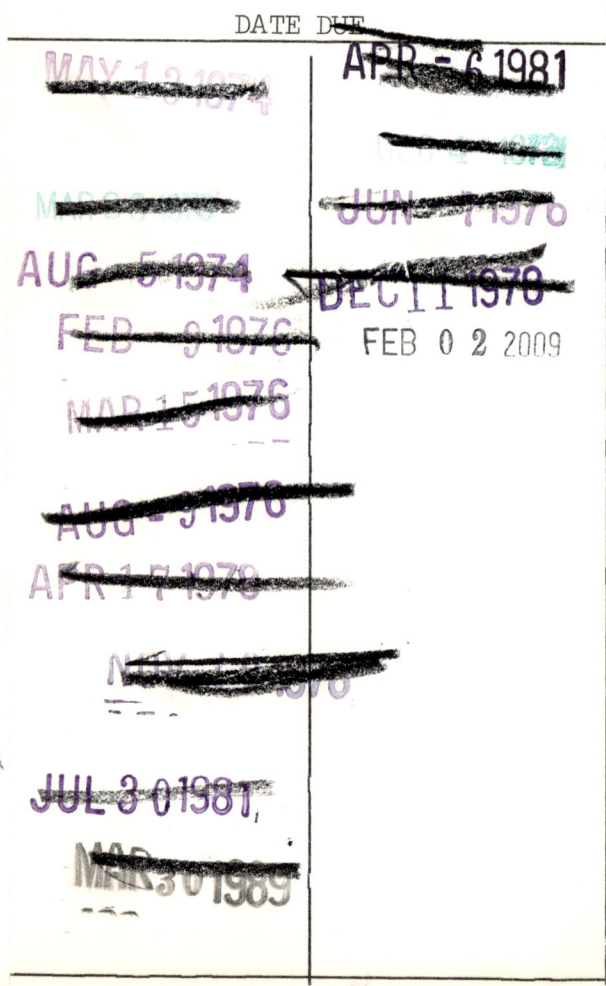